French-American Genealogical Research
Monograph Number 2, Parts 1 and 2

EMIGRANTS FROM FRANCE
(HAUT-RHIN DEPARTEMENT)
TO AMERICA

PART 1: 1837–1844
PART 2: 1845–1847

Clifford Neal Smith

CLEARFIELD

Part 1 originally published
McNeal, Arizona, 1986

Part 2 originally published
McNeal, Arizona, 1989

Reprinted, two parts in one volume, for
Clearfield Company, Inc. by
Genealogical Publishing Co., Inc.
Baltimore, Maryland
2004

International Standard Book Number: 0-8063-5232-9

Made in the United States of America

EMIGRANTS FROM FRANCE (HAUT-RHIN DEPARTEMENT)

TO AMERICA, PART 1: 1837-1844

Clifford Neal Smith

First printing, November 1986   √ʃ
Reprint, October 1988   qz
Reprint, September 1989   qz
 Reprint, April 1990   u
 Reprint, April 1991   qz
Reprint, December 1992   qz

INTRODUCTION

This monograph begins a subseries (1837-1857) in which the emigrants from the Upper Alsace (Departement du Haut-Rhin) to the United States are set forth. Herein, will also be found the names of a few persons who, although foreigners, received passports from the Haut-Rhin departmental government.

The populace of the Upper Alsace descends predominantly from the German tribes which settled the area in late Roman times. Their underlying language is a Swabian (Alemannic) dialect of German closely related to the dialects of Baden, Switzerland, and Wuerttemberg. Today, however, the official language is French, but German is still to be heard, particularly in rural areas. In the list which follows, the collision of languages and cultures is reflected in the surnames, some being Germanic in origin, others French.

The Upper Alsace (or Sundgau) was historically a family possession of the Habsburgs and, therefore, *Reichsunmittelbar*--a "direct" part of the Holy Roman Empire, German Nation; the practical effect of which was payment of taxes directly to the imperial government, rather than to an intermediate prince. For the peasants and bourgeoisie, this "direct" status also meant that they were serfs and subjects of the Habsburg emperors. After the Treaty of Westphalia in 1648 the free cities of the Upper Alsace, including Colmar and Mulhausen (Mulhouse), fell to France. Thus, the populace of the Upper Alsace remained mainly Catholic. Down through the centuries, the region has been under both German and French administrations, thus creating a certain cultural ambivalence in the Alsatian populace not seen elsewhere in either France or Germany.

The following list of emigrants has been extracted from registers 7 and 8 of passports issued by the departmental government for travel outside of France. (The whereabouts of the first six registers is not known to this writer.) Most of the entries in these registers record travel to European cities, and thus are not of direct interest to American genealogical researchers. However, there may be exceptions in that trips made to ports, such as Hamburg, or to London, may have been only intermediate destinations in unreported emigration to America. Consequently, a number of such entries have also been included herein. The registers are to be found in the Archives Departementales du Haut-Rhin in Colmar; they have been microfilmed by the Genealogical Society of Utah on microfilm roll 1,069,294.

It is perhaps of genealogical interest to note that, inserted in the front cover of register 7, is a loose page with the letterhead of the Prefeture du Bas-Rhin, Strasburg, dated 13 March 1843, addressed to the Prefet of Haut-Rhin, Colmar, containing the following notation:

> "Judith Levy, wife of ... Wolf Wollenberger of Hirsingen (and) Regine or Reine, widow of David Stern of Higesheim, expelled from Wuerttemberg."

* * * * *

The entries hereinafter are arranged in three lines:

First line: Volume (registers 7 or 8) and entry number and date of entry.

Second line: Name of emigrant, age, and profession; accompanying family members.

Third line: Place of birth, place of residence (at time passport was issued), and destination.

Register 7
(1 Jul 1837 to 30 Jun 1842)

7:012   11 Jul 1837
BAILLEY, Thiebaut, age 32, farmer; with wife & children
St.-Germain   St.-Germain   New York

7:013   11 Jul 1837
ROTH, Chretien, age 31, farmer
Dornach   Heimsbrunn   New York

7:022   15 Jul 1837
PAQUOT, Pierre Francois Xavier, age 52
Bethonsvillier   Bethonsvillier   New York

7:047   02 Aug 1837
DREYFOUS, Jules, age 20, merchant
Belfort   Belfort   New Orleans

7:060   09 Aug 1837
DOMINE, Francois, age 40, farmer; with wife & 2? children
Chavannes-les-   Chavannes-les-   New York
  Grands   Grands

7:061   09 Aug 1837
PY?, Joseph, age 49
Le-Cetain   Le-Cetain   New York

7:063   09 Aug 1837
CHOMANN, Francois Xavier, age 37, shoemaker
Wiedensohlen   Wiedensohlen   New Orleans

7:069   12 Aug 1837
BIDEAUX, Francoise, age not given, daylaborer (Woman?)
Villars-le-Sec   Villars-le-Sec   USA

7:112   11 Sep 1837
GRAFF, Mathias, age 29, landowner
Colmar   Colmar   New York

7:116   13 Sep 1837
MEYER, Francois Antoine, age 24, potter?
Niederlarg   Niederlarg   Philadelphia

7:133   28 Sep 1837
RITZENTHALER, Andre, age 51, farmer; with 2 sons
Huntzenheim   Huntzenheim   New York

7:140   05 Oct 1837
MEYER, Jean, age 30, carpenter
Wickerswihr   Wickerswihr   Philadelphia

7:145   11 Oct 1837
DURBAN, Barbe, age 28, factory worker (woman)
Duerrenentzen   Colmar   New York

7:149   12 Oct 1837
FLEITH, Antoine, age 50, farmer
Riedwihr   Wiedwihr   Philadelphia

7:211   20 Dec 1837
GAUCHET, Alexis? (Alexander?), age 31, gardener
Dorand   Dorand   New York

7:245   12 Feb 1838
EGENSCHWILLER, Xavier, age 27, wheelwright
Winckel   Winckel   New York

7:249   16 Feb 1838
HOFER, Jean, age 38, carpenter
Mulhausen   Mulhausen   London

7:275   06 Mar 1838
PELTIER?, Etienne, age 46, daylaborer; with wife & 4 children
Salbert   Salbert   New Orleans

7:276   06 Mar 1838
EGLIN, Jean, age 33, daylaborer
Mulhausen,   Obermichelbach   New York
  Baden

7:277   06 Mar 1838
RUPP, Jean, age 58, farmer
Orschweyer,   Orschweyer,   New York
  Baden   Baden

7:279   06 Mar 1838
MOINET, Francois, age 42, foilmaker (lamier)
Denney   Denney   New York

7:280   07 Mar 1838
DREYFOUS, Daniel, age 43, businessman
Paris   Belfort   New Orleans

7:282   07 Mar 1838
JUENN, Christian, age 52, mason; with wife & 4 children
Schruntz,   Belfort   New York
  Austria

7:283   10 Mar 1838
ROSSELOT, Henry, age 40, carpenter; with wife & 6 children
Andelmans   Andelmans (or   New York
                     Belfort)

7:292   15 Mar 1838
AMSTUTZ, Pierre, age 22, farmer
Leymen   Mulembert?   New York

7:298   22 Mar 1838
STRASZEWICZ, Alexandre, age 24, Polish refugee
--? Poland   Guebwiller   London

7:300   23 Mar 1838
KAUFFMANN, Jacques, age 38; with wife & 4 children
Hirtzbach   Staffelfelden   New York

7:301   23 Mar 1838
KAUFFMANN, Chretien, age 31, with wife
Hirtzbach   Staffelfelden   New York

7:304   26 Mar 1838
SCHOELLHAMMER, Eduard, age 28, mechanic
Strasbourg   Mulhausen   London

7:305   26 Mar 1838
BOCK, Henry, age 41, businessman
Dessau, An-   Dessau or Mul-   London
halt, Germany   hausen

7:315   30 Mar 1838
MAUDRIN, Jean Jacques, age 22, cooper
Moval?   Moval?   New York

7:332   18 Apr 1838
ROOS, Edouard, age 20, locksmith?
Masseraux   Masseraux   New York

7:345   23 Apr 1838
TENNETTE, Leopold, age 42, farmer
Liepvre?   Liepvre?   New Orleans

7:346   23 Apr 1838
STOECKLE, Jacques, age 22, locksmith
Soppe-le-Bas   Soppe-le-Bas   New York

7:348   24 Apr 1838
STOLTZ, Ignace, age 51, joiner; with wife & 6 chil-
dren
Buehl, Baden   Massevaux   New York

7:359   28 Apr 1838
JEHLEN, Thiebaud, age 51, coachman? (coucher); with
wife & 8 children
Guebwiller   Guebwiller   New York

7:360   28 Apr 1838
SCHMELTZ, Francois Antoine, age 54, turner; with
wife & 1 son
Wille?   Wille?   New York
(Wiele?) Bohe-   (Wiele?), Bohe-
mia   mia

7:363   28 Apr 1838
ROSSELOT, Jean Pierre, age 36, landowner
Vourvenans?   Vourvenans?   New York

7:375   04 May 1838
KARRER, Jeanne, age 29; wife of Pierre CSEHIRRET?
Soppe-le-Haut   Soppe-le-Haut   New York

7:384   11 May 1838
DIETRICH, Thiebaud, age 55, landowner; with wife, 3
children, & son-in-law
Soppe-le-Haut   Soppe-le-Haut   New York

7:392   17 May 1838
BAUMLER, Jean, age 44, draper; with wife & step-
daughter
Buehl   Buehl   New York

7:396   21 May 1838
GRIESSER, Louis, age 21, painter? --?
Thann   Thann   New ?

7:399   23 May 1838
DITNER, Paul, age 30, shoemaker
Burnhaupt-   Burnhaupt-   New York
le-Bas   le-Bas

7:400   23 May 1838
BITSCH, Jean, age 24, daylaborer
Burnhaupt-   Burnhaupt-   New York
le-Bas   le-Bas

7:428   09 Jun 1838
WALLSCHMIT, Jean Nepomucene, age 25, tailor; with
wife
Guebwiller   Lautenbach   New York

7:433   12 Jun 1838
NORROT, Dominique, age 21, farmer
Bourogne   Bourogne   New York

7:434   13 Jun 1838
VOLANT, Nicolas, age 37, baker; with wife & 2 chil-
dren
Nancy   Belfort   New York

7:436   13 Jun 1838
OCHS, Jean, age 31, businessman
Mulhausen   Dornach   London

7:456   28 Jun 1838
GOEPFERT, Leger, age 25, blacksmith
Guemar   Guemar   Philadelphia

7:472   09 Jul 1838
BOSSLER, Francois, age 17, factory worker; with brother Ignace, age 19
Bourbach-   Issenheim   Schibenville,
le-Bas   America

7:474   10 Jul 1838
ROESCH?, Prothais, age 29, farmer
Guemar   Guemar   Philadelphia

7:479   12 Jul 1838
SCHACHERER, Joseph, age 34, daylaborer
Traubach-   Traubach-   New York
le-Haut   le-Haut

7:488   20 Jul 1838
HOLTZ, Jean, age 27, shoemaker
Muehlhausen,   Waldighoffen?   New York
  Baden

7:489   20 Jul 1838
SCHMITT, Joseph, age 22, shoemaker
Waldighoffen   Waldighoffen   New York

7:513   30 Jul 1838
GERIG, Barbe, age 60, daylaborer (woman); with son,
  age 24
Wintzenheim   Staffelfelden   New York

7:532   08 Aug 1838
BLUM? (BLUNE?), Marie, age 31, daylaborer
Eloge? (Eloye?) Eloge? (Eloye?) New York

7:547   14 Aug 1838
ALBERT, Jean Baptiste, age 19, weaver? (tissier)
Liepvre   Liepvre   New Orleans

7:548   14 Aug 1838
FETTAT?, Louis, age 30, weaver? (tissier)
Liepvre   Liepvre   New Orleans

7:549   14 Aug 1838
RUYER, Marie Sara, age 27, weaver? (tissier)
Liepvre   Liepvre   New Orleans

7:550   14 Aug 1838
KNOLL, Jean Baptiste, age 40, warper (in weaving)
Liepvre   Liepvre   New Orleans

7:551   14 Aug 1838
MERCIOLE, Jean Baptiste, age 31, weaver? (tissier)
Liepvre   Liepvre   New Orleans

7:552   14 Aug 1838
URBAIN, Joseph, age 25, weaver? (tissier)
Liepvre   Liepvre   New Orleans

7:553   14 Aug 1838
BOLF, Francois, age 23, weaver? (tissier)
Liepvre   Liepvre   New Orleans

7:554   14 Aug 1838
GUILLAUME, Joseph, age 20, worker
Liepvre   Liepvre   New Orleans

7:555   14 Aug 1838
LASSIAT, Sebastien, age 22, worker
Liepvre   Liepvre   New Orleans

7:564   18 Aug 1838
BARBIER, Sebastien, age 36, signalman
Liepvre   Liepvre   New Orleans

7:571   24 Aug 1838
HANNISIERE, Marguerite, age 25, weaver
Lallemand-   Lallemand-   New York
Rombach   Rombach

7:572   24 Aug 1838
FEIL, Jean Baptiste, age 30, weaver
Lallemand-   Lallemand-   New York
Rombach   Rombach

7:573   24 Aug 1838
LAGRESSE? (LAGUESSE?), Jean Dominique, age 30,
  weaver
Lallemand-   Lallemand-   New York
Rombach   Rombach

7:585   31 Aug 1838
FLEURENT, Marguerite, age 30, daylaborer
Et   Liepvre   New Orleans

7:588   31 Aug 1838
DELAFIELD, --?, age 18, student
London   Colmar   London

7:594   04 Sep 1838
KOINCE, Francois, age 25, domestic
Suarce   Suarce   USA

7:595   04 Sep 1838
GOFFINET, Francois, age 27, shoemaker
Boron   Boron   New York

7:599   08 Sep 1838
CURIE, Ferdinand, age 48, normal school professor
Montbeliard,   Colmar   London
  Doubs

7:602   10 Sep 1838
KOCH, Jean George, age 20, wheelwright
Liepvre   Liepvre   New Orleans

7:603   10 Sep 1838
VILLEMIN, George, age 19, farmer
Liepvre   Liepvre   New Orleans

7:640   28 Sep 1838
GRAFF, Jeremias?, age 25, businessman?
Mulhouse   Mulhouse   London

7:643   01 Oct 1838
MIGEON, Jules, age 24, master blacksmith
Mezire,   Mezire,   London
  Haut-Rhin   Haut-Rhin

7:648   04 Oct 1838
VOGEL, George, age 25, mason
Wydensohlen   Wydensohlen   USA
  (Wiedensohlen) (Wiedensohlen)

7:649   04 Oct 1838
VOGEL, Martin, age 22, farmer
Wydensohlen   Wydensohlen   New Orleans
  (Wiedensohlen)   (Wiedensohlen)

7:654   08 Oct 1838
BUECHER, Joseph, age 30, hosier (bonnetier)
Widensohlen   Widensohlen   New Orleans
  (Wiedensohlen)   (Wiedensohlen)

7:655   08 Oct 1838
VOGEL, Jean Baptiste, age 21, daylaborer
Guemar   Guemar   New York

7:661   08 Oct 1838
GUTLEBEN, Jean Baptiste, age 33, weaver; with wife
Wiedensohlen   Wiedensohlen   New Orleans

7:665   13 Oct 1838
STOFFEL, Andre, age 28, daylaborer; with wife & 2
  children
Wiedensohlen   Wiedensohlen   New Orleans

7:670   19 Oct 1838
DELE? (DETE?), Joseph, age 32, weaver? (tissier)
Liepvre   Liepvre   New Orleans

7:671   15 Oct 1838
ANTZMANN, Jean Baptiste, age 33, daylaborer; with
  wife
Liepvre   Liepvre   New Orleans

7:677   23 Oct 1838
DOMINIQUE, Philippe, age 39, baker
Lallemand-   Liepvre   New Orleans
  Rombach

7:691   06 Nov 1838
DUVIC, Joseph, age 44, farmer; with wife (Marie Ann
  APPE) and son Jean PP., age 16
Liepvre   Liepvre   New Orleans

7:739   07 Jan 1839
KREYER, Francois Xavier, age 35, tailor
Roderen   Belfort   New Orleans

7:752   25 Jan 1839
GAIFFE, Nicolas, age 41, engraver?
Besancon   Mulhausen   London

7:753   25 Jan 1839
CHAPPUIS, Jean Marie, age 38, mechanic
Lons-le-   Mulhausen   London
  Saulnier

7:761   06 Feb 1839
GEIGER, Joseph, age 28, architect
Mulhausen   Mulhausen   London

7:763   07 Feb 1839
CREVOISERAT, Joseph, age 15, eclesiastic?
Delle   Delle   New York

7:765   09 Feb 1839
VAUTHIER, Jean Pierre, age 28, miner
Chatenois,   Chatenois   New York
  Haut-Rhin

7:766   09 Feb 1839
GRASSELER, Francois Xavier, age 34, farmer; with
  wife & 3 children
Rougegoutte   Rougegoutte   New York

7:768   14 Feb 1839
ROTH, Nicolas, age 19, factory worker
Wuerclingen?,   Dornach   Ohio, America
  Baden

7:769   14 Feb 1839
GOLDSCHMIDT, Joseph, age 30, farmer
Ste.-Marie-   Dornach   Ohio, America
  aux-M(ines)

7:771   16 Feb 1839
LANGENFELD, Martin, age 26, carpenter
Wiedensohlen   Wiedensohlen   Philadelphia

7:773   21 Feb 1839
BOEGLIN, Xavier, age 31, daylaborer; with wife, mo-
  ther-in-law, & 2 children
Manspach   Altenach?   New York

7:774   21 Feb 1839
MARCHAND, Antoine, age 23, miner
Chatenois   Chatenois   New York

7:783   02 Mar 1839
GROSJEAN, Etienne, age 23, --?
Dorans   Dorans   New York

7:784   02 Mar 1839
SONTE, Isau Pierre, age 25, --?
Bellemagny   Bellemagny   New York

7:785   02 Mar 1839
HENNEMAN, George, age 60, weaver; with wife & nephew
Rougegoutte   Rougegoutte   New York

7:786   04 Mar 1839
SCHLEGEL, Michael?, age 30, farmer
Frannigen?   Mulhausen   New York

7:787   04 Mar 1839
BOHRER, Jean Baptiste, age 35, tailor
Willer   Mulhausen   New York

7:789   04 Mar 1839
OBRECHT, Madeleine, age 16, maid
Colmar   Colmar   USA

7:790   04 Mar 1839
DEMEUSY, Mathias, age 24, mason
Puix   Puix   New York

7:791   04 Mar 1839
COLIN, Jacques, age 32, woodcutter
Puix   Puix   New York

7:793   05 Mar 1839
ROTH, Jean, age 41?, farmer
Pulvertheim?   Mulhausen   New York

7:795   08 Mar 1839
ROTH, Nicolas, age 25, farmer; with wife
Remberville?   Landser?   New York

7:796   08 Mar 1839
ROTH, Chretien, age 35; with wife, 4 children, &
  sister-in-law
Lorguin,   Jeannemarie?   New York
  Meurthe?

7:799   09 Mar 1839
CHASSIGUET, Joseph, age 17, tailor
Puix   Puix   New York

7:801   12 Mar 1839
DICK? (RICK?), Anne, age 18, domestic
Altkirch   Mulhausen   New York

7:805   14 Mar 1839
OBRECHT, Jacques, age 27, baker
Jebsheim   Jebsheim   Philadelphia

7:814   19 Mar 1839
ESCHAINE, Joseph Damien, age 28, farmer
St. Cohne?   St. Cohne?   New York

7:815   21 Mar 1839
ANCEL, Francois, age 39, farmer
Liepvre   Liepvre   New Orleans

7:816   21 Mar 1839
BARBIER, Marie Barbe, age 25, weaver? (tissiere)
Liepvre   Liepvre   New Orleans

7:817   21 Mar 1839
GRELOT, Marie Rose, age 21, dressmaker
Senonne?   Senonne?   New Orleans

7:819   22 Mar 1839
KREYBULL, Jacques, age 36, laborer; with wife & 3
  children
Dampierre-   Belfort   New York
  Outre-le-Bois,
  Doubs

7:820   22 Mar 1839
KREYBULL, Jean, age 45, laborer; with wife & 4 chil-
  dren
St. Susanne,   St. Susanne,   New York
  Doubs   Doubs

7:828   30 Mar 1839
ROCK?, Joseph, age 34, mason; with wife
Oberstexbach?, Liepvre   New Orleans
  Bas-Rhin

7:829   30 Mar 1839
LUTIGUE?, George, age 48, farmer
Breitenau,   Liepvre   New Orleans
  Bas-Rhin

7:830   30 Mar 1839
GRUSS?, Antoine, age 35, mason; with wife & 5 chil-
  dren
Velvisheim?,   Liepvre   New Orleans
  Bas-Rhin

7:831   30 Mar 1839
NECK, George, age 26, carpenter
Liepvre   Liepvre   New Orleans

7:832   30 Mar 1839
GERMAIN, Francois, age 35, farmer
Liepvre   Liepvre   New Orleans

7:833   30 Mar 1839
COLLIN, Jean Baptiste, age 20, farmer
Liepvre   Liepvre   New Orleans

7:834   30 Mar 1839
MENETRE, Antoine, age 35, weaver? (tissier); with
  wife & 2 children
Liepvre   Liepvre   New Orleans

7:835   30 Mar 1839
JACQUOT, Joseph, age 38, farmer; with wife
Liepvre   Liepvre   New Orleans

7:837   02 Apr 1839
FOHRER?, Francois Antoine, age 39, shoemaker; with
  wife
Traubach Haut? Traubach Haut? New York

7:838   02 Apr 1839
JEANNEZ, Joseph, age 20, shoemaker
Bretagne   Bretagne   New York

7:841   02 Apr 1839
ANDRE, Michel, age 31, farmer
Liepvre   Lallemand-   USA
                  Rombach

7:844   04 Apr 1839
HORNY, Sebastien, age 33, laborer; with wife, 2
  children, & brother-in-law
Guebwiller   Guebwiller   New York

7:845   04 Apr 1839
LUTTENBACHER, Andre, age 34, metal worker; with 2
    children, mother-in-law, & sister-in-law
Guebwiller   Guebwiller   New York

7:846   04 Apr 1839
FAIVRE, Jean Pierre, age 19, farmer
Rechotte   Rechotte   New York

7:847   05 Apr 1839
SCHMITT, Joseph, age 28, metal worker
Guebwiller   Guebwiller   New York?

7:849   06 Apr 1839
KOCH, Antoine, age 28, farmer
Liepvre   Liepvre   New Orleans

7:850   08 Apr 1839
STOCKHAUSEN, Francois, age 48, --?; with wife & mo-
    ther? (niece?) D(omini)que BILDSTEIN
Cologne?   Guebwiller   London

7:853   10 Apr 1839
SPRATLER, Antoine, age 63, laborer; with wife & 4
    children
Guemar?   Guebwiller   New York

7:856   10 Apr 1839
GASPERMENT, Jean Francois, age 26, laborer
La-Coutte?   Labouille   Philadelphia
    (Coiulte?),
    com(mune?) Ste.-
    Croix-aux-Mines

7:857   12 Apr 1839
BOSSERT, Mathieu, age 31, farmer; with wife, 1
    child, & brother? (brother-in-law?)
Guebwiller   Guebwiller   New York

7:859   13 Apr 1839
HAUSER?, Francois Joseph, age 38, landowner
Altkirch   Altkirch   New York

7:871   19 Apr 1839
MASSON, Nicolas, age 37, farmer
Freland?   Ste.-Croix-   Philadelphia
                  aux-Mines

7:872   20 Apr 1839
WEISS, Mathias, age 26, --?
Mulhausen   Mulhausen   Rotterdam

7:878   22 Apr 1839
COLLIN, Jean Francois, age 36, farmer
Lallemand-   Lallemand-   USA
Rombach   Rombach

7:886   26 Apr 1839
ZETTER, Adele, age 23, teacher
Mulhausen   Mulhausen   London

7:888   29 Apr 1839
WILLY, Joseph, age 19, weaver; with brother Pierre
Mortzwiller   Mortzwiller   New York

7:895   02 May 1839
LEROMAIN, Alexandre, age 31, weaver? (tissier)
Liepvre   Liepvre   New Orleans

7:900   04 May 1839
ROOS, Conrad, age 49, locksmith; with 5 children
Massevaux   Massevaux   New York

7:901   04 May 1839
MANSBENDEL?, Frederic, age 18, draftsman?
Mulhausen   Mulhausen   London

7:904   06 May 1839
KOECHLIN, Isaac, age 26, manufacturer
Willer   Willer   London

7:905   07 May 1839
BOERLEN, Apollinaire, age 31, daylaborer; with wife,
    3 children, & sister-in-law
Burnhaupt-   Burnhaupt-   New York
le-Bas   le-Bas

7:910   13 May 1839
SENTER, Guillaume, age 23, farmer
Burnhaupt-   Burnhaupt-   New York
le-Bas   le-Bas

7:912   13 May 1839
AFFHOLDER, Jean Pierre, age 21, daylaborer
Burnhaupt-   Burnhaupt-   New York
le-Bas   le-Bas

7:913   13 May 1839
KIRCHER, Jacques, age 23, daylaborer
Burnhaupt-   Burnhaupt-   New York
le-Bas   le-Bas

7:914   13 May 1839
HEGY, Sigismond, age 29, daylaborer
Burnhaupt-   Burnhaupt-   New York
le-Bas   le-Bas

7:921   16 May 1839
KOCH, Jean Baptiste, age 33, butcher; with wife
    Marie Madelene, & 1 child
Liepvre   Liepvre   New Orleans

7:930   21 May 1839
BITSCH, Francois Joseph, age 48, weaver
Burnhaupt-   Burnhaupt-   New York
le-Bas   le-Bas

7:931   21 May 1839
HAGER, Ambroise, age 28, daylaborer
Schweighausen   Schweighausen   Quebec, Canada

7:934   25 May 1839
KLEINFELD, Joseph, age 33, farmer; with wife
Guebwiller   Guebwiller   New York

7:957   04 Jun 1839
KIRSCHER, Francois Joseph, age 31, farmer
Burnhaupt-   Burnhaupt   New York
  le-Bas

7:994   26 Jun 1839
RUETER, Jean Baptiste?, age 32, woodworker; with
  wife
Cernay   Guebwiller   New York

7:1012   02 Jul 1839
JULLERAD, Jean Pierre, age 46, blacksmith?; with
  wife & 1 child
Magny   Staffelfelden   New York

7:1033   15 Jul 1839
WEINZAEPFLIN, Romain, age 26, theological student
Ungersheim   Ungersheim   Philadelphia

7:1037   20 Jul 1839
ROUECHE? (RUECHE?), Jean Pierre, age 20
Brebatte?   Brebatte?   New York

7:1087   19 Aug 1839
HAUTZ, Jean Pierre, age 33, daylaborer; with wife &
  2 children
Rechotte?   Rechotte?   New York

7:1088   19 Aug 1839
PULCHER, Martin, age 33, innkeeper; with wife, 7
  children, & brother
Chaux   Chaux   New York

7:1089   19 Aug 1839
BELOT, Francois Xavier, age 37, farmer
Sermamagny   Sermamagny   New York

7:1110   28 Aug 1839
BISCHOFF, Thiebaud, age 59, farmer; with wife & 6
  children
Cernay   Cernay   New York

7:1134   16 Sep 1839
ZIMMERMANN, Salome, age 21, normal school teacher
Ste.-Croix-   Ste.-Croix-   USA
  en?-Plan?   en?-Plan?

7:1137   17 Sep 1839
KLOPPSTEIN, Chretien, age 19, --?
Belfort   Florimont?   New York

7:1144   19 Sep 1839
SLUDER, Catherine, age 26, musician; with son & aunt
Burnhaupt-   Burnhaupt-   New York
  le-Bas   le-Bas

7:1147   23 Sep 1839
REISS, Jacques, age 46, butcher
Bouxwiller,   Cernay   New York
  Bas-Rhin

7:1149   25 Sep 1839
HEITZ, Antoine, age 44, woodturner?; with wife & 4
  children
Burnhaupt-   Burnhaupt-   New York
  le-Bas   le-Bas

7:1151   28 Sep 1839
SAUVAGEOT, Jacques, age 19, farmer
Lamadelaine   Etueffon-Bas   New York

7:1152   30 Sep 1839
ENTZ, Ignace, age 41, farmer; with wife & 3 children
Rouffach   Rouffach   Jeffersons, Amer-
                                    ica

7:1159   04 Oct 1839
COURANT, Laurent Eduard, age 38, businessman
Poissi?,   Mulhausen   New York
  --? Oise

7:1160   09 Oct 1839
HINZINGER, Therese, age 45, (wife of Jacques MAR-
  TIN); with 6 children
Fouchy,   Liepvre   New Orleans
  Bas-Rhin

7:1170   11 Oct 1839
STAUFFER, Joseph, age 20, laborer
Altkirch   Richwiller?   Ohio, America

7:1171   11 Oct 1839
SCHLATTER, Sebastien, age 20, laborer
Richwiller   Pfastatt   Ohio, America

7:1179   16 Oct 1839
CHOMAR? (THOMAR?), Nickel?, age 28, carpenter; with
  wife & 2 children
--?   Bitschwiller?   New York

7:1181   24 Oct 1839
WEIMER? (WUMER?), Pierre, age 24, farmer
Janfrey/Doubs   Berrwiller?   USA

7:1182   24 Oct 1839
KLEIN, Thiebaud, age 24, daylaborer
Straets? --?   Bitschwiller   New York

7:1183   24 Oct 1839
PRAELKE? (PRAETKE?), Albert, age 45, carpenter; with
  son
Breme Ville   Thann   New Orleans
  Libre*
  *Probably Freistadt Bremen, Germany, is meant.

7:1184   24 Oct 1939
SCHMITT, Jean, age 38, carpenter; with wife & 4
    children
Hitterswiller?, Thann   New Orleans
  Bas-Rhin

7:1185   24 Oct 1839
ERDMANN, Chretien, age 43, shoemaker; with wife &
    daughter
Ritzingen?,   Guebwiller   Philadelphia
  Bas-Rhin

7:1187   25 Oct 1839
DEYLE? (DREYLE?), Prax, age 23, wooden shoemaker
Etueffon-Haut   Etueffon-Haut   New York

7:1189   28 Oct 1839
ERNIE, Frederic?, age 28, spinner; with wife & 3
    children
Oberseebach,   Thann   New York
  Bas-Rhin

7:1197   29 Oct 1839
AMSTUTZ, Joseph, age 20, farmer
Leymen?   Grandwiller?   New York

7:1203   07 Nov 1839
BOESCHLIN, Georges, age 20, butler (or wine celler-
    man)
Andisheim   Andisheim   London

7:1235   27 Nov 1839
SCHMITT, Conrad, age 20, farmer
Oberdorff   Oberdorff   New York

7:1236   27 Nov 1839
FEDERSPIEL?, Augustin, age 20, musician?
Bisel   Bisel   New York

7:1238   28 Nov 1839
ORLOWSKI, Casimir, age 34, refugee
Warsaw   Eutisheim?   London

7:1259   10 Dec 1839
BLAISE?, Gigos? (or GIGOT?, Blaise?), age 41, car-
    penter
Bisel   Bisel   New Orleans

7:1260   10 Dec 1839
BURTSCHER, Jean, age 24, farmer
Bisel   Bisel   New Orleans

7:1261   14 Dec 1839
RUPP, Chretien, age 21, domestic; with sister?
Reinbeck   Folgensburg   New York
  Langhalter?
  --

7:1263   16 Dec 1839
SCHMITT, Pierre, age 25
Oberdorff   Oberdorff   New York

7:1265   16 Dec 1839
LEHMES, Jean, age 23, shepherd
Koettlach?   Koettlach?   New Orleans

7:1266   19 Dec 1839
SCHMITT, Joseph, age 23, shoemaker
Waltighoffen? Waltighoffen?   New York

7:1267   21 Dec 1839
BISANTZ, Pierre, age 40, former teacher
Steinsaltz   Steinsaltz   New York

7:1270   23 Dec 1839
KEIFLIN, Charles, age 35, daylaborer; with wife & 1
    child
Vieux? Fer-   Vieux? Fer-   New York
  rette   rette

7:1271   23 Dec 1839
BRUN, Bernhard, age 41, carpenter; with wife, 4
    children, & 2 nephews
Ferrette   Ferrette   New York

7:1272   23 Dec 1839
KESSLER, Blaise, age 68, carpenter; with daughter &
    3 children
Oltingen?   Oltingen?   New York

7:1276   27 Dec 1839
BECK, Jean Baptiste, age 47, daylaborer; with wife &
    5 children
Vieux Fer-   Vieux Fer-   New York
  rette   rette

7:1277   30 Dec 1839
STOECKLEN, Pierre, age 27, daylaborer
Soppe-le-Bas   Soppe-le-Bas   New York

7:1281   02 Jan 1840
ROTH, Andre, age 18, carpenter
Oltingen   Oltingen   New York

7:1283   03 Jan 1840
ROTH, Nicolas, age 54, worker; with wife & 4 chil-
    dren
Pulvertheim?   Dornach   Ohio, America

7:1295   17 Jan 1840
BOESCH, Jean Caspar, age 55, dyer
Neslau,   Colmar   Charleston
  Switzerland

7:1297   22 Jan 1840
DE POUVOURVILLE, Adolphe, age 29, businessman
Mulhausen   Mulhausen   Texas

7:1298   22 Jan 1840
SPRATTLER, Antoine, age 34, laborer; with wife & 2
    children
Guemar   Guebwiller   New York

7:1299   22 Jan 1840
MUNSCH, Fortune, age 30, daylaborer; with wife & 2
   thildren
Heinersdorff   Dornach   Ohio, America

7:1300   22 Jan 1840
FIESSINGER, Joseph, age 30, carpenter; with wife, 2
   children, brother-in-law, & domestic
Rimbachzell   Guebwiller   New York

7:1303   23 Jan 1840
ORTSCHEIDT, Andre, age 30, farmer
Vieux Fer-   Vieux Fer-   New York
   rette   rette

7:1304   25 Jan 1840
SCHUSSELE, Jean Georges, age 55, wheelwright
Reichenbach,   Guebwiller   New York
   Baden

7:1305   25 Jan 1840
BILGER, Michel, age 28, weaver
Riespach?   Riespach?   New York

7:1306   27 Jan 1840
DROXLER, Antoine, age 25, carpenter
Riespach?   Riespach?   New York

7:1310   30 Jan 1840
BAUBEZ, Germain, age 33, farmer; with wife & 3 chil-
   dren
Offemont   Offemont   Louisville, Amer-
                                 ica

7:1311   30 Jan 1840
CUENOT, Antoine, age 46, farmer; with wife & 4 chil-
   dren
Offemont   Offemont   Louisville, Amer-
                                 ica

7:1312   30 Jan 1840
RIPON, Jacques, age 30, tailor; with wife & 1 child
Offemont   Offemont   Louisville, Amer-
                                 ica

7:1313   30 Jan 1840
MILLER, Joseph, age 19, farmer
Chavannette?   Chavannette?   New York

7:1316   01 Feb 1840
FELES? (FETES?), Louis, age 19, teacher
Offemont   Offemont   Louisville, Amer-
                                 ica

7:1317   01 Feb 1840
GCHWIND (properly GSCHWIND), Jean, age 40, tailor
Hindlingen   Hindlingen   New York

7:1319   04 Feb 1840
FOLLOT, Francois Xavier, age 25, tailor
(none)   Offemont   Louisville, Amer-
                                 ica

7:1320   04 Feb 1840
PERREZ, Marguerite, age 27
Offemont   Offemont   Louisville, Amer-
                                 ica

7:1328   10 Feb 1840
DROZ, Jean Claude, age 19, weaver
Chaux   Chaux   New York

7:1329   10 Feb 1840
POMMIER, Joseph, age 29, farmer; with sister & maid
Chaux   Chaux   New York

7:1330   10 Feb 1840
LAUGARD? (LANGARD?), Joseph, age 45, farmer; with
   wife & daughter
Chaux   Chaux   New York

7:1333   13 Feb 1840
COURTOT, Jean Pierre, age 34, farmer
Chatenois   Chatenois   New York

7:1334   13 Feb 1840
RESET, Francois, age 40, confectioner
Charmois   Delle   New York

7:1341   19 Feb 1840
BUFFLER, Marguerite, age 27 (wife of Joseph SCHMITT)
Guebwiller   Guebwiller   New York

7:1342   20 Feb 1840
TSCHIRREL?, Pierre, age 19, farmer
Soppe-le-Haut Soppe-le-Haut New York

7:1343   21 Feb 1840
MURES? (MURER?), Guillaume, age 21, woodturner
Burnhaupt-   Burnhaupt   New York
   le-Bas

7:1350   24 Feb 1840
RIMBOLD, Joseph, age 19, carpenter; with sister
Leval?   Leval?   Philadelphia

7:1351   24 Feb 1840
MOULIN, Jean Pierre, age 52, farmer; with wife & 4
   children
Rougemont   Rougemont   Philadelphia

7:1352   24 Feb 1840
PETITJEAN, Jean Pierre, age 30, farmer; with wife &
   3 children
Rougemont   Rougemont   Philadelphia

7:1353   24 Feb 1840
LAMBELIN, Pierre, age 42, farmer; with wife & 6
   children
Rougemont   Rougemont   Philadelphia

7:1354   24 Feb 1840
DUPONT, Jean Claude, age 61, farmer; with 2 children
Rougemont   Rougemont   Philadelphia

7:1355   24 Feb 1840
GEANT, Jean Pierre, age 35, farmer; with wife & 3
   children
Rougemont   Rougemont   Philadelphia

7:1356   24 Feb 1840
MOULIN, Pierre, age 24, farmer; with wife & 2? chil-
   dren
Rougemont   Rougemont   Philadelphia

7:1357   24 Feb 1840
BLANC, Georges, age 47, farmer; with wife & 4 chil-
   dren
Rougemont   Rougemont   Philadelphia

7:1358   24 Feb 1840
DUPONT, Jean Claude, age 29, farmer; with wife & 1
   child
Rougemont   Rougemont   Philadelphia

7:1361   26 Feb 1840
KUENEMANN, Pierre, age 27, mason; with brother
Mortzwiller   Mortzwiller   New York

7:1362   26 Feb 1840
VEYH, Jean Michel, age 19, daylaborer
Soppe-le-Haut   Soppe-le-Haut   New York

7:1363   26 Feb 1840
KOECHIN, Adolphe, age 20, chemist
Jungbunzlau,   Mulhausen   Manchester (Eng-
  Bohemia   land?, America?)

7:1365   28 Feb 1840
KOCH, Ferdinand, age 32, farrier
Linthal   Lautenbachzell New York

7:1368   29 Feb 1840
GIRARDEY, Nicolas, age 30, farmer; with wife & 1
   child
Rouge Goutte   Rouge Goutte   New York
  (Rougegoutte)   (Rougegoutte)

7:1370   07 Mar 1840
DIDIER, Thiebaut, age 37, farmer; with wife, 4 chil-
   dren, & maid
Etueffaut-Haut Etueffaut-Haut New York

7:1371   07 Mar 1840
BELET, Francois?, age 23, shoemaker; with wife
Rougemont   St. Germain   New York

7:1372   07 Mar 1840
SCHOFFA, Ignace, age 27, farmer
Koestlach   Koestlach   New York

7:1379   09 Mar 1840
SCHMITT, Jean, age 27, daylaborer
Mittelmuespach? Mitelmuespach? New York

7:1380   09 Mar 1840
MONNIER, Jean Baptiste, age 25, wheelwright
Etouffout-Haut Etueffout-Haut New York

7:1382   10 Mar 1840
PREVOT, Pierre, age 24, farmer
Chaux   Chaux   New York

7:1388   14 Mar 1840
RIVEZ, Francois Georges, age 32, farmer
Chaux   Chaux   New York

7:1398   19 Mar 1840
WEBER, Marie Anne, age 30
Oberdorff   Oberdorff   New York

7:1400   20 Mar 1840
MINETREZ, Jean Pierre, age 18, carpenter
Magny   Faveron   New York

7:1402   23 Mar 1840
WITT, Charles, age 30, farmer
Seppois-le-Bas Seppois-le-Bas Philadelphia

7:1403   23 Mar 1840
OSSER?, Jacques, age 30, butcher
Biederthal   Biederthal   New York

7:1413   27 Mar 1840
BERNI, Joseph, age 21, silversmith?
Calice --?   Calice   Hamburg
  (Italy?)

7:1419   02 Apr 1840
KUTTLER, Sebastien, age 34, weaver; with wife & 1
   child
Sternenberg   Diefmatten   New York

7:1420   02 Apr 1840
LORENTZ, Joseph, age 24, weaver
Sternenberg   Sternenberg   New York

7:1422   03 Apr 1840
SAUSSOTTE, Francois, age 41, farmer; with wife & 8
   children
Etueffout-Haut Petit-Magny   New York

7:1424   04 Apr 1840
SIEGFRIED, Jean, age 17, business agent
Mulhausen   Mulhausen   Mexico

7:1425   04 Apr 1840
JAEGY, Jean, age 22, businessman?
Riespach   Riespach   New York

7:1426   04 Apr 1840
KEMPF, Jean Thiebaut, age 27, domestic
Uberstratt   Uberstratt   New York

7:1427   04 Apr 1840
HAAS, Marie-Rose, age 24, dressmaker
Rimbach   Guebwiller   New York

7:1429   06 Apr 1840
BENNER?, Louise, age 32, dressmaker
Minetter?   Guebwiller   New York

7:1430   06 Apr 1840
MOUREAUX, Jacques, age 26, mechanic's aide
Delle   Guebwiller   New York

7:1432   06 Apr 1840
JACQUEMIN, Nicolas Emile, age 59, mechanic's aide
Senouer?,   Guebwiller   New York
  Vosges

7:1433   06 Apr 1840
ABDORFF? (OBDORFF?), Jacques, age 20, mechanic's
  helper
Guebwiller   Guebwiller   New York

7:1434   06 Apr 1840
BONNERONT, Jacques, age 32, farmer; with wife & 1
  child
Weinbourg,   Weinbourg? or   New York
  Bas-Rhin   Guebwiller

7:1435   06 Apr 1840
LENLART?, Jean-Adam, age 26, farmer
Wingen,   Wingen or   New York
  Bas-Rhin   Guebwiller

7:1437   06 Apr 1840
BILDSTEIN, Louis-Henri-Alexandre, age 22, mechanic's
  helper
Guebwiller   Guebwiller   New York

7:1439   08 Apr 1840
HOIGNE, Jean-Jacques, age 25, manufacturer of chemi-
  cal products
Vellescot   Vellescot   New York

7:1440   08 Apr 1840
BRAND, Boniface, age 46, carpenter; with wife & 5
  children
Burnhaupt-Haut   Burnhaupt-Haut New York

7:1446   11 Apr 1840
ENDERLIN, Henri, age 39, cylinder maker; with wife
Courtavon   Courtavon   Philadelphia

7:1454   16 Apr 1840
ZIEGLER, Johann?, age 27, mechanic's aide; with wife
  & 2 children
Endingen,   Guebwiller   New York
  Baden

7:1455   16 Apr 1840
LINSENBOLTZ?, Jean, age 39, woodturner; with wife, 2
  children, & servant
Krautergerts-   Guebwiller   New York
  heim, Bas-Rhin

7:1459   17 Apr 1840
CUISINIER, Marie-Jeanne, age 34, designer
Velescot   Velescot   New York

7:1460   18 Apr 1840
BORTMANN, Jean-Baptiste, age 38, farmer; with wife,
  2 children, & servant
Eschholtzmatt   Blotzheim   New York

7:1462   21 Apr 1840
SCHITTLY, Jean, age 40, coachman; with wife & 6
  children
Falckwiller   Cernay   New York

7:1463   21 Apr 1840
GILGENKRANTZ? (GILGENKRAUTZ?), Jean-Baptiste, age
  34, manufacturer of --?
Sigolsheim   Cernay   New York

7:1464   21 Apr 1840
KIRSCHER, Joseph, age 58, oil merchant?; with wife &
  5 children
Burnhaupt-Bas   Burnhaupt-Bas   New York

7:1471   21 Apr 1840
SICHEL, Francois Joseph, age 40, weaver; with wife &
  2 children
Memelshoffen?   Wiretzhausen?   New York
  (Meuelshoffen?)

7:1472   23 Apr 1840
GREINER, Jean, age 40, weaver?; with wife & 2 chil-
  dren
Moutron,   Namsheim   New York
  Moselle

7:1474   23 Apr 1840
TRIBIS, Charles, age 37, mechanic
Wasselomm?   Moernach?   New York
  Bas-Rhin

7:1475   23 Apr 1840
MULLER, Marie-Ursulle, age 47, wife of Henri HERZOG
Seppois-le-Bas   Moos   New York

7:1478   24 Apr 1840
BORNMANN, Jean Frederic, age 24, locksmith
Ste.-Marie-   Ste. Marie   New York
  aux-M(ines)

7:1479   24 Apr 1840
GOETZ, Jean, age 28, pharmacist
Altkirch   Ferrette   New Orleans

7:1486   29 Apr 1840
JOBERT, Isidore, age 41, designer
Belfort   Mulhausen   London

7:1489   04 May 1840
KIRSCHER, Francois Joseph, age 41, carpenter?
Burnhaupt-Bas   (not given)   New York

12

7:1490   04 May 1840
KIRSCHER, Francois? Joseph?, age 32, farmer; with
    sister
Burnhaupt-Bas   (not given)   New York

7:1493   04 May 1840
TREIBER, Boniface, age 38, farmer
Burnhaupt-Haut   (not given)   New York

7:1496   05 May 1840
WALEDIECH?, Bernard, age 24, businessman
Ferrette   Ferrette   New Orleans

7:1497   05 May 1840
MARSOT, Philippe, age 40, domestic
La-Cote,   Mulhausen   Cincinnati, Amer-
  Haute-Saone   ica

7:1498   05 May 1840
GOETZ, Jean, age 30, blacksmith
Walldorf,   Guebwiller   New York
  Nassau

7:1499   05 May 1840
ROOSZ, Mansedus?, age 22, blacksmith
Burnhaupt-Bas   Burnhaupt   New York

7:1500   05 May 1840
WEISS, Francois Joseph, age 37, weaver; with wife
Burnhaupt-Bas   Burnhaupt   New York

7:1504   05 May 1840
WERLIN, Francois, age 25, cooper
Delle   Delle   New York

7:1505   06 May 1840
HUEBER, Gaspar, age 19, calico? printer
Ranspach?   Ranspach   Baltimore

7:1506   06 May 1840
GISSY, Joseph, age 19, calico? printer
Ranspach?   Ranspach   Baltimore

7:1507   06 May 1840
WOLFART, Anne Marie, age 40; with 2 children
Soppe-le-Bas   Soppe-le-Bas   New York

7:1508   06 May 1840
HIRTH, Catherine, age 52; with son & maid
Soppe-le-Bas   Soppe-le-Bas   New York

7:1512   07 May 1840
EGLY, Jacques, age 24
Soppe-le-Bas   Soppe-le-Bas   New York

7:1515   07 May 1840
BERO? (BERS?), Joseph, age 47, farmer; with wife, 4?
    children, & brother-in-law
Ste.-Croix-   Bruebach   New York
  aux-Mines

7:1516   07 May 1840
MULLER, Joseph, age 55, farmer; with wife & 4 chil-
    dren
Lebene,   Geispitzen   New York
  Vosges

7:1520   09 May 1840
LUTRINGER, Marie Anne, age 20; with sister
Hutteren?   Ste.-Omarin?   Augusta, America

7:1521   09 May 1840
ORTH, Chretien Philippe, age 64, foundry worker;
    with wife & 4 children
Loerrath,   Hartmanswiller   New York
  Baden (Loerrach?)

7:1526   12 May 1840
BOURGUARDEZ, Francois? (or Francoise?), age 22
Soppe-le-Bas   Soppe-le-Bas   New York

7:1530   13 May 1840
DITNER, Joseph, age 39, daylaborer; with 8 children
Burnhaupt   Burnhaupt-Haut   New York

7:1535   18 May 1840
KUPPELMEYER, Jean Louis, age 54, locksmith
Lauterbourg   Guebwiller   New York

7:1536   18 May 1840
ROLAND, Alphonse, age 23, coachmaker? (coachman?)
Delle   Delle   New York

7:1538   18 May 1840
DUPLAIN, Pierre Joseph, age 27, baker
Grandvillars   Delle   New York

7:1548   22 May 1840
JAEGLEN, Jean, age 25, daylaborer
Gafingen?   --?   New York
  (Gafinger?)

7:1550   23 May 1840
GEIGER, Ambroise, age 29, daylaborer
Burnhaupt-   (none)   New York
  le-Haut?

7:1551   23 May 1840
DAVID, Benoit, age 34, farrier
Bourg-et-   Ste.-Marie-   New Orleans
  Bruch?   a(ux) M(ines)

7:1553   23 May 1840
CALLEY, Newlad?, age 19, farmer
Faverois   Faverois   New York

7:1563   29 May 1840
ROTH, Jean, age 42, --?; with wife, 3 children, &
    brother-in-law
(none)   Landtor?   New York

7:1579   03 Jun 1840
DIHLES, --?, age 30, businessman
Altkirch   Altkirch   New York

7:1580   03 Jun 1840
SILBERMANN, Blaise, age 22, butcher
Bernwiller   Bernwiller   New York

7:1585   06 Jun 1840
BENOIT, Joseph, age 26, farmer
Ste.-Marie-   Ste.-Marie   New Orleans
  aux-Mines

7:1588   10 Jun 1840
DILNER? (DITNER?), Thiebaut, age 31, printing fore-
  man
Ounnertzwiller Ounnertzwiller New York

7:1590   10 Jun 1840
HATTENBERGER, George, age 19, baker
Soppe-le-Haut   Soppe   New York

7:1591   10 Jun 1840
CHRISTEN, Pierre, age 24, locksmith
Balschwiller   Balschwiller   New York

7:1602   12 Jun 1840
ITTEL, David, age 36, farmer
Sundhoffen   Harbourg   New York

7:1620   17 Jun 1840
BOSSARD, Joseph, age 50, tenant? farmer; with wife &
  4 children
Hunawihr?   Hautgauen?   New York

7:1628   29 Jun 1840
JEISCH, Francoise-Antoine, age 36, teacher
Mulhausen   Mulhausen   New York

7:1632   02 Jul 1840
GIGAUDET, Jean-Pierre, age 42, farmer
Meroux   Meroux   New York

7:1648   04 Jul 1840
ROTHENBURGER, Jean Baptiste, age 33, farmer
Rauffach   Rauffach   Jeffersons, Amer-
                                   ica

7:1658   07 Jul 1840
STAFFELBACH, Joseph, age 41, signalman; with wife &
  2 children
Wettolsheim   Ittenheim   Mexico

7:1661   07 Jul 1840
WAPLER, Frederic Guillaume, age 50, businessman
Strasbourg   Mulhausen   New Orleans

7:1662   07 Jul 1840
WAPLER, Emile, age 20, businessman
Strasbourg   Mulhausen   New Orleans

7:1677   13 Jul 1840
KELLERMANN, Chretien Charles, age 35, locksmith
Ste.-Marie-   Ste.-Marie-   New Orleans
  aux-M(ines)   aux-M(ines)

7:1688   17 Jul 1840
BERNARD, Jean Pierre, age 20, commercial agent
Faverois   Faverois   New York

7:1700   25 Jul 1840
RIFFART, Charles-Etienne, age 45, saddler; with wife
  & 3 children
Rheinfeld,   Belfort   New York
  Prussian Rhineland

7:1714   29 Jul 1840
RUECHE, Pierre-Francois, age 18, manufacturer
Brebotte   Brebotte   New York

7:1716   30 Jul 1840
BASS? (BAST?), Mathieu, age 22, farmer
Rouffach   Rouffach   Jeffersons, Amer-
                                   ica

7:1724   03 Aug 1840
BURY, Jean, age 25, saddler
Gildwiller   Gildwiller   New York

7:1736   07 Aug 1840
HILLENMEYER, Remy Xavier, age 25, gardener
Wattwiller   Cernay   New York

7:1745   13 Aug 1840
SERGER, Charles, age 27, businessman
Carlsruhe   Mulhausen   London

7:1750   14 Aug 1840
KRUST, Thiebaud, age 26, farmer
Aspach-le-Bas   Aspach-le-Bas   New York

7:1757   17 Aug 1840
CALLEY? (CATTEY?), Veronique, age 26
Faverois   Faverois   New York

7:1758   17 Aug 1840
CHARPIAT, Mathias, dit (called) George, age 21
Faverois   Faverois   New York

7:1836   28 Sep 1840
EICKER?, Jean, age 20, farmer
Bisel   Staffelfelden   New York

7:1841   09 Oct 1840
MASSEY?, Ludan?, age 31, carpenter
Marlenheim,   Thann   New York
  Bas-Rhin

7:1843   09 Oct 1840
MALLER? (MULLER?), Aug(ust) Ch--?, age 35, music
  teacher; with sister
Colmar   Colmar   St. Louis, America

14

7:1852   12 Oct 1840
RICH, Jacques, age 19, farmer
Bourtzwiller   Bourtzwiller   New York

7:1907   11 Nov 1840
NASENFORDER? (HASENFORDER?), Georges, age 47, sadd-
  ler
St.-Louis   St.-Louis   New York

7:1921   26 Nov 1840
BOTT, Louis, age 22, carpenter
Ribeauville   Ribeauville   New York

7:1986   10 Feb 1841
RISLER, Mathieu, Junior, age 25, businessman
Cernay   Cernay   London

7:1989   11 Feb 1841
KOCH, Philippe, age 44, baker
Guebwiller   Guebwiller   New York

7:1997   16 Feb 1841
ESCHLIMANN, Pierre, age 23, --? political refugee
Willer   Willer   New York

7:2000   22 Feb 1841
KREYSCHER, Elisabeth, age 27, wife of SCHLETZER?;
  with 2 children
Ste.-Marie-   Ste.-Marie-   New Orleans
  a(ux)-M(ines)   a(ux)-M(ines)

7:2008   25 Feb 1841
NAFZGER, Pierre, age 35, daylaborer; with wife (age
  24)
Walheim   Galfingen   New York

7:2011   25 Feb 1841
LICHTY, Jacques, age 38, domestic; with son (age 6?)
Bettendorff   Altkirch   New York

7:2026   05 Mar 1841
GOERIG, Joseph, age 41, farmer
Bourg, Vosges   Ste.-Marie-   Ohio, America
                    a(ux)-M(ines)

7:2027   05 Mar 1841
JUNG, Philippe Jacques, age 27, carpenter
Ste.-Marie   Ste.-Marie-   New Orleans
                    a(ux)-M(ines)

7:2028   05 Mar 1841
LEBERT?, Jean Baptiste, age 51, designer
Legelbach?   Mulhausen   London
  (Logelbach?)

7:2033   09 Mar 1841
FLEURY, Simon, age 29, spinner
St.-Dizier   Cernay   New York

7:2034   09 Mar 1841
SCHNEIDER, Joseph, age 53, daylaborer; with family
Carspach?   Carspach?   New York

7:2035   09 Mar 1841
EBERLIN, Jean, age 33, daylaborer; with family
Carspach?   Carspach?   New York

7:2037   10 Mar 1841
DELARUE, Michel, age 29, spinner
Esch, Switzer-   Mulhausen   Richemond (Rich-
  land   mond), America

7:2039   11 Mar 1841
SCHUMACHER, Jean Michel, age 22, daylaborer
Kunheim   Munster   New York

7:2040   11 Mar 1841
DREHER, Frederic, age 54, carpenter; with family
Annweiller,   Ste.-Marie-   New Orleans
  Bas-Rhin   a(ux)-M(ines)

7:2041   11 Mar 1841
WINCKELMANN, Frederic, age 20, cooper --?
Montbeliard,   Belfort   New York
  D(oubs)

7:2043   16 Mar 1841
HIMBERT, Joseph, age 50, farmer; with wife
Aspach   Offemont   New York

7:2052   19 Mar 1841
JODER, Jacques, age 62, farmer; with wife, 3 daugh-
  ters, sister, brother-in-law, & 2 nephews
Hirsingen   Hirsingen   New York

7:2057   22 Mar 1841
FINKBOHNER?, Frederic, age 27, --? (moucher)
Bard?   Ribeauville   New York

7:2061   25 Mar 1841
HAENERLE, George, age 39, farmer; with family
Duren   Entzen   Wahren Wahren
                                      (Warren?),
                                      America

7:2062   25 Mar 1841
MURBACH, Jean, age 39, farmer; with family
Kunheim   Kunheim   New York

7:2063   25 Mar 1841
HUNSINGER?, Jean? Baptiste?, age 24, farmer
Kunheim   Kunheim   New York

7:2064   26 Mar 1841
LASCHE?, Antoine, age 28, farmer
Guemar   Guemar   Philadelphia

7:2065   26 Mar 1841
ROESCH? (ROESLE?), Francois Louis, age 21, baker
Guemar   Guemar   Philadelphia

7:2066   26 Mar 1841
DIDION, Jean --?, age 23, farmer
Guemar   Guemar   Philadelphia

7:2070   29 Mar 1841
ALBERT, Marie Jeanne, age 26, factory worker
Liepvre   Liepvre   New Orleans

7:2071   29 Mar 1841
COLLEGNON, Marie Rose, age 22, factory worker
Liepvre   Liepvre   New Orleans

7:2076   01 Apr 1841
WERTH, Blaise, age 33, constable? (connetier)
Hirsingue   Hirsingue   New York

7:2077   02 Apr 1841
DREY, Antoine, age 18, weaver
Duren   Entzen   New York

7:2088   05 Apr 1841
ZIMMERMANN, Jean, age 49, (tenant?) farmer; with
     family
Hegenheim   Hegenheim   Zinzinnati (Cin-
                                cinnati), Amer-
                                ica

7:2089   05 Apr 1841
ZUBER?, Frederic, age 38, businessman
Rinheim?   Rinheim?   London

7:2091   08 Apr 1841
ROTHMUND, Joseph?, age 45, mason; with son Pierre
Mulhafen, Baden Guebwiller   New York

7:2098   1 Apr 1841
RADELSPERGER, David, age 14
Illhaeusern   Illhaeusern   New York

7:2099   13 Apr 1841
FRANC? (FRANE?), George, age 26, farmer
Perouse   Perouse   New York

7:2107   13 Apr 1841
LISCHER, Jean Baptiste?, age 24, carpenter
Kunheim   Kunheim   Warren, America

7:2110   14 Apr 1841
KLOPFENSTEIN, Jean?, age 53, (tenant?) farmer; with
     family
Florimont   Florimont   New York

7:2111   14 Apr 1841
MARCHAL, Pierre J(osep)h, age 32, farmer
Suarce   Suarce   New York

7:2125   17 Apr 1841
POURCHE, Ferdinand, age 18, farmer
Perouse   Perouse   New York

7:2127   19 Apr 1841
HESSER, Philippe, age 27, factory worker
Muntzenheim   Muntzenheim   New York

7:2131   20 Apr 1841
KUENTZ, Jacques, age 29, carpenter
Bouxwiller   Bouxwiller   New York

7:2132   20 Apr 1841
STEINBACH, Georges, age 32, manufacturer
Mulhausen   Mulhausen   London

7:2135   21 Apr 1841
BLECH? (BLECK?), Frederic, age 33, manufacturer
Mulhausen   Mulhausen   London

7:2136   21 Apr 1841
MONNIER, Francois? --?, age 46; with family
Suarce   Suarce   New York

7:2156   04 May 1841
JOBERT, Isadore, age 42, designer
Belfort   Mulhouse   London

7:2160   07 May 1841
CONTI, Ambroise, age 29, jeweler
Val de Mouz-   Belfort   Hamburg
   zela?, Italy

7:2166   08 May 1841
SOMME, Jean, age 22, carpenter; with sister
Schlestadt?   Schlestadt? (or   New York
                   Illhaeusern)

7:2176   13 May 1841
SCHOELLHAMMER, Eduard, age 31, mechanic
Strasbourg   Strasbourg (or   London, via Am-
                   Mulhouse)   sterdam

7:2177   13 May 1841
SOMMER, J(osep)h?, age 24, carpenter?
Jebstadt   Jebheim?   New York

7:2181   17 May 1841
AUGUSTI, Catherine, age 24
Bouxwiller   Illhaeusern?   New York

7:2184   18 May 1841
KROPF, Henry, age 29, --?; with wife, 1 child, &
     brother
(illegible)   Illhaeusern?   New York

7:2198   25 May 1841
SCHWEIGHOFER, J(osep)h, age 55, entrepreneur
Vienna, Austria Mulhausen   London

7:2261   27 Jun 1841
MERMOT, Pierre, age 21, carpenter?; with wife & 1
    child
Belfort   Belfort   New York

7:2266   27 Jun 1841
RITTNER, Jean, age 24, blacksmith
Andolsberg?   Andolsberg?   New York

7:2275   05 Jul 1841
ZURCHER, Charles, age 22, commercial agent
Mulhouse   Mulhouse   London

7:2288   15 Jul 1841
KOCHLIN Gustave, age 29, manufacturer
Mulhausen   Mulhausen   New York

7:2291   15 Jul 1841
LEFEBVRE, Eugene, age 33, landowner?
Havre   Orbey   London

7:2296   16 Jul 1841
HERZOG, Antoine, age 55, --?
Dornach   Logelbach   London

7:2312   29 Jul 1841
REIS?, --, Mme.?, nee JOHVETTEL?, age 41, butcher
Strasbourg   Cernay   New Orleans

7:2330   05 Aug 1841
DEISS, Frederic, age 17, ropemaker
Bouxwiller   Vieux-Thann   New Orleans

7:2358   20 Aug 1841
BURGUNDER, Pierre, age 31, carpenter
Morcken? (or   Sohn? (or   New Orleans
   Morckensohn?)   Morckensohn?)

7:2359   20 Aug 1841
DUMET, Joseph, age 27, tinsmith
Olpe, Prussia   Thann   New York

7:2360   20 Aug 1841
ZEPPENFELD, Francois, age 41, tanner?
Olpe, Prussia   Thann   New York

7:2365   24 Aug 1841
HEINIS, Francois Joseph, age 47, dentist; with wife
Habsheim   Thann   New York

7:2408   21 Sep 1841
WOLPLER? (WOLFLER?), Oscar, age 17, business agent
Strasbourg   Mulhausen   New Orleans

7:2409   21 Sep 1841
WOLPLER, Fred(eric) --?, age 51, businessman
Strasbourg   Mulhouse   New Orleans

7:2410   21 Sep 1841
LURY?, Jean, age 21, commercial agent
Colmar   Mulhouse   New Orleans

7:2419   28 Sep 1841
WALTER, Martin, age 53, gardener; with family
Felleringen?   Felleringen?   New Orleans

7:2442   22 Oct 1841
MONDRUX?, Francois, age 30
Woval?   Woval?   Louisville,
                                         America

7:2452   04 Nov 1841
BRUNTZ, Laurent, age 24, locksmith?
Didenheim?   Didenheim?   Philadelphia
  (Dedenheim?)   (Dedenheim?)

7:2460   09 Nov 1841
CONTI, Francesco A., age 19, domestic; with Stephano
Cardarola,   Cardorale?   Hamburg
   Varm?

7:2461   09 Nov 1841
BELLI, Battista, age 29, musician; with nephew --?
   --?
Moranti/W   Moranti   Hamburg

7:2465   11 Nov 1841
SENGEL?, Jean, age 42, carpenter
Ste.-Marie-   Ste.-Marie-   New York
   a(ux)-Mines   a(ux)-Mines

7:2479   20 Nov 1841
GRENTZINGER?, --, age 45, farmer; with family
Steinsaltz   Steinsaltz   New York

7:2498   18 Nov 1841
JODER, Joseph, age 20, farmer
Tagsdorff?   Hirtzbach   New York

7:2499   18 Nov 1841
JODER, Chretien, age 20, farmer
Kargitzen?   Heunersdorff?   New York
  (Zargitzen?)

7:2510   05 Jan 1842
MOLLY, Antoine, age 32, confectioner
Colmar   Colmar   New York

7:2511   07 Jan 1842
EDEL, Georges, Junior?, age 28, carpenter?
Ribeauville   Ribeauville   London

7:2519   15 Jan 1842
RAPINE, Madeleine, age 27
Villars   --?   New York

7:2520   17 Jan 1842
BLIND?, Gregoire?, age 21, blacksmith?
Kiffis   Kiffis   New York

7:2521   17 Jan 1842
BLIND, Francois? J(osep)h?, age 22, blacksmith?
Kiffis   Kiffis   New York

7:2535   29 Jan 1842
REINHARD, David, age 46, weaver; with wife & 2 chil-
    dren
Algolsheim   Algolsheim   New York

7:2539   02 Feb 1842
WAGLER, Jean, age 31, farmer; with wife, 1 child, &
    servant
Ribeauville   Ribeauville   New York

7:2540   07 Feb 1842
FIRET, --, Mme., nee GERENTAL? age 28; with 3
    children
Beaucourt   Beaucourt   New York

7:2560   07 Mar 1842
GIRARDEY, Francois J(osep)h, age 39, former --?;
    with family
Hirsingen   Hirsingen   Augusta, America

7:2566   10 Mar 1842
BURGUNDER, Sophie Marie, Mme., age 28
Storcken?   Sohn?   New Orleans
  (Storckensohn?)   (Storckensohn?)

7:2567   10 Mar 1842
THRO?, Francoise, Mme., age 30; with 1 child
Urbes   Urbes   New Orleans

7:2568   11 Mar 1842
STEMMELEN, Mathieu, age 31, farmer
Balschwiller?   Balschwiller?   New York

7:2572   14 Mar 1842
CEUTLIVRE? (CUTLIVRE?), Marie, age 28
Lutran?   Lutran?   New York
  (Sutran?)   (Sutran?)

7:2575   16 Mar 1842
HALLER, Michel, age 23, carpenter
Felleringen   Felleringen   New Orleans

7:2576   17 Mar 1842
GWUERTZ, Nicolas, age 37
Felleringen   Felleringen   New Orleans

7:2579   22 Mar 1842
OBRECHT?, Michel, age 39, laborer; with wife & 5
    children
Jebsheim   Jebsheim   New York

7:2599   02 Apr 1842
ITTEL, Marie Salome, age 28, servant
Horbourg   Horbourg   New York

7:2607   09 Apr 1842
ERDMANN, Francois?, age 45, bargeman; with daughter
    Cath(erine)
Gungwiller?,   Guebwiller   Philadelphia
  Bas-Rhin

7:2612   12 Apr 1842
ZUBER, Frederic, age 39, businessman
Rischeim   Rischeim   London

7:2617   12 Apr 1842
BUMB? (BUML?), Sebastien, age 31, tailor
Kemlingen?,   Colmar   Cincinnati,
  Bavaria   America

7:2618   12 Apr 1842
SUTTEBEN? (SUTLEBEN?), Antoine, age 28, farmer
Wiedensohlen?   Wiedensohlen?   New Orleans

7:2623   20 Apr 1842
JELSCH, Joseph, age 26, tanner
Hirsingen   Hirsingen   New York

7:2625   20 Apr 1842
HOEFFLIGER, Valentin, age 32, turner of --?
Guebwiller   Guebwiller   New York

7:2635   27 Apr 1842
HUBSCHNEIDER? (HUBSCHWERLIN?), Francois Antoine, age
    31, harness maker
Hirsingen   Hirsingen   New York

7:2636   28 Apr 1842
MUETH, Jean, age 24, domestic
Bisel   Bisel   New York

7:2637   28 Apr 1842
BURGUNDER, Pierre, age 23, laborer
Sondersdorff   Sondersdorff   New York

7:2647   03 May 1842
HANHART, J. J., age 40, commercial agent
Mulhouse   Thann   London

7:2655   06 May 1842
HALLER, Antoine, age 29, daylaborer
Felleringen   Felleringen   New Orleans

7:2656   06 May 1842
KREYENBUHL, J(osep)h?, age 37, cabinetmaker; with
    family
Durenentzen?   Mulhouse   New York

7:2662   12 May 1842
DOLLFUS, Jean, age 42, manufacturer
Mulhausen   Mulhausen   London

7:2677   17 May 1842
PETIT, --, age 60, widow of Jean Michel (PETIT), nee
   WAGNER
Mulhouse   Mulhouse   St. Louis, Amer-
                                      ica

7:2683   18 May 1842
IMBES, Antoine, age 37, -- (cottier?); with family
Wolschwiller   Wolschwiller   New York

7:2684   18 May 1842
JUEN, Anne Marie, age 21
Wolschwiller   Wolschwiller   New York

7:2686   18 May 1842
CONTI, Ambroise, age 30, jeweler
Val d'Mar-   Belfort   Hamburg
   zala, Italy

7:2693   21 May 1842
MAECHLER?, Ignace, age 47, manufacturer
Sigolsheim?   Sigolsheim?   New York

7:2694   23 May 1842
HANHART, Michel, age 33, --?
Wihr-en-Plaine?   Andolsheim   New York

7:2702   26 May 1842
SOLARI, Orlando, age 21, organ player
(none)   Belfort   Hamburg

7:2712   30 May 1842
BORNMANN, Jean Jacques, age 21, saddler
Ste.-Marie-   Ste.-Marie-   New Orleans
   a(ux)-Mines   a(ux)-Mines

Register 8

8:0039   24 Jun 1842
DOPLER, Cath(erine) Therese, age 29
Niederhag-   (Niederhag-   New York
   en(thal?)   en?)thal
(Note: Niederhagen is written in one column and Thal
in the other; it is not known whether one village
name is meant, or two.)

8:0070   11 Jul 1842
SCHULTZ, Pierre, age 54, landowner
Hunnigen   Hunigen?   London

8:0082   20 Jul 1842
BLECH, Frederic, age 33, manufacturer
Mulhouse   Mulhouse   London

8:0104   30 Jul 1842
BOBAY? (ROBAY?), Jean Pierre, age 43, daylaborer;
   with 4 children
St.-Germain   St.-Germain   New York

8:0107   01 Aug 1842
KOENIG, Georges, age 34, weaver
Carspach   Carspach   Philadelphia

8:0109   02 Aug 1842
HAMBERGER, Pierre George August Ros., age 42, --?
Biesheim   Colmar   London

8:0120   08 Aug 1842
DONIAT?, Pierre, age 21, mechanic
Mezire   Mezire   New York

8:0139   17 Aug 1842
NAMZE?, Jacques, age 32, professor
Ireves?   Mulhouse   London
   (Treves?)

8:0174   31 Aug 1842
HUMMEL, Catherine, age 25, servant
Bergheim   Bergheim   Philadelphia

8:0209   16 Sep 1842
BURCKBUCHLER, Francois Antoine, age 34, worker
Hatten   Bitschwiller   New York

8:0224   26 Sep 1842
HAGENBACH, Meinrad, age 30, waiter --?
Niedermond-   Guebwiller   London
   willer?

8:0252   20 Sep 1842
SCHUH, Jean Baptiste, age 28, farrier
Liepvre   Liepvre   New Orleans

8:0254   22 Sep 1842
BANGARD, Jean Francois, age 18, woodturner
Liepvre   Liepvre   New Orleans

8:0256   22 Sep 1842
GREINER, --, nee HYLANDT, age 32; with daughter
Muhlbach   Hundwihr?   New York
                      (Hunawehr?)

8:0258   26 Sep 1842
FREIHARD, Jean Baptiste, age 22, carpenter
Liepvre   Liepvre   New Orleans

8:0259   27 Sep 1842
CHARBONNIER, Antoine, age 38, civil engineer
Laon   Mulhouse   London

8:0288   22 Oct 1842
LECLAIRE, Jean Baptiste, age 62, threader?
Rientzheim   Colmar   London

8:0292   24 Oct 1842
FORSTER, N(icol)as?, age 20, mason
Mortzwiller   Mortzwiller   New York

8:0293   24 Oct 1842
STEINER, Jacques, age 18, commercial agent
Mulhouse   Mulhouse   London

8:0326   24 Nov 1842
SCHWARTZ, Joseph, age 29, baker
Pfaffenheim   Pfaffenheim   New York

8:0329   29 Nov 1842
SOMMEREISEN, Jean Baptiste, age 32, farmer; with
     wife & 2 children of tender age
Rouffach   Rouffach   Schefferson
                                  (Jefferson?)
                                  City, USA

8:0330   29 Nov 1842
PROBST, Francois Barnabe, age 26, farmer
Rouffach   Rouffach   Schefferson
                                  (Jefferson?)
                                  City, USA

8:0331   29 Nov 1842
FAUST, Jean Baptiste, age 25, farmer
Rouffach   Rouffach   Schefferson
                                  (Jefferson?)
                                  City, USA

8:0340   04 Jan 1843
BLANC, Laurent, age 45, --?; with wife & 3? children
Eloy   Eloy   Louisville,
                                  America

8:0350   25 Jan 1843
PULCHER, Claude Jacques, age 64, farmer
Chaux   Chaux   New York

8:0353   26 Jan 1843
FRIEZ, Joseph, age 23
Boron   Boron   New York

8:0374   08 Feb 1843
GRASBOILLOT? (GRUSBOILLOT?), Jean, age 20, farmer
St.-Germain   St.-Germain   New York

8:0375   08 Feb 1843
TAVERNIER, Pierre Francois, age 27, farmer; with his
--? Jean Baptiste GIRARD
ST.-Germain   St.-Germain   New York

8:0383   13 Feb 1843
SCHAEFFOLDT, Jean Baptiste, age 37, landowner
Ribeauville   Ribeauville   New York

8:0390   18 Feb 1843
SCHWEITZER,, Jean,, Jean, age 23, saddler
Hesingue?   Hesingue?   New York

8:0391   20 Feb 1843
SCHENEBERG, Pierre, age 24, carpenter
--orance?   --orance?   New York

8:0402   01 Mar 1843
FRETZ, Andre, age 28, --?
Belfort   Valdoye   New York

8:0412   06 Mar 1843
TELE? (FELE?), Louis, age 56
Offemont   Offemont   New York

8:0417   13 Mar 1843
DIDIER, Jean Claude, age 28, farmer
St.-Germain   St.-Germain   New York

8:0418   13 Mar 1843
RICHARD, Charles, age 46, businessman
Mulhausen   Mulhausen   New Orleans

8:0422   16 Mar 1843
NACHBAUR, Pierre, age 42, businessman
Cernay   Cernay   New York

8:0431   23 Mar 1843
MOSER, Benoit, age 43, farmer
Bollwiller?   Muehlhausen   New York
                 (Mulhausen?)

8:0435   25 Mar 1843
REINHARD, Jean Ulric, age 36, farmer & cattle dealer
Illzach   Illzach   York, America

8:0441   27 Mar 1843
COURTOT? (COURLOL?), Jacques, age 38, farmer
Offemont   Offemont   New York

8:0453   30 Mar 1843
ROESS, Jean, age 22, --?
Wintzenheim   Wintzenheim   New York

8:0455   01 Apr 1843
MARSOT, Celestine, age 27; with sister Cheren? MAR-
SOT, age 20
Boron   Boron?   New York

8:0457   01 Apr 1843
BRAUN, Matthieu, age 33, dyer
Mulhausen   Mulhausen   New York

8:0458   04 Apr 1843
MATTLER, Joseph, age 44, daylaborer
Dirlinsdorff   Dirlinsdorff   New York

8:0462   05 Apr 1843
SPRATTLER, Francois Joseph, age 27, daylaborer
Guemar   Guebwiller   New York

8:0473   12 Apr 1843
KRAFFT, Laurent, (age not given), laborer
--? Raedersheim Raedersheim   New York

8:0480   15 Apr 1843
RICH, Pierre, age 47, tenant farmer
Montjoie   Neuwiller?   New York

8:0482   15 Apr 1843
EICHER, Jacques, age 55, farmer
Heiteren?   Heiteren?   New York

8:0499   26 Apr 1843
MULLER, Thiebaut, age 44, cooper --?
Rouffach   Rouffach   New Orleans

8:0522   09 May 1843
WEBER, Michel, age 40, farmer
Rouffach   Rouffach   Schefferson
                                (Jefferson?),
                                America

8:0596   21 Jun 1843
SAUVAGEOT, Xavier, age 18, farmer
Lamadelaine   Etueffont-Bas New York

8:0613   30 Jun 1843
MUELLER, Jean, age 23, carpenter
Kaysersberg   Kaysersberg   New Orleans

8:0615   01 Jul 1843
RISLER, Mathias, Senior, age 60, manufacturer & may-
    or of Cernay
Mulhausen   Cernay   London

8:0658   26 Jul 1843
DARVEL, Claude, age 44, designer
Lyon   Mulhausen   London

8:0665   31 Jul 1843
GROS RENAUD, Charles, age 38, designer
Mulhausen   Mulhausen   London

8:0669   04 Aug 1843
JOBERT, Isidore, age 44, designer
Belfort   Mulhausen? (or London
                 Belfort?)

8:0676   09 Aug 1843
NIEDERHAUSER, Jacques, age 20, landowner
Mulhausen   Mulhausen   London

8:0680   11 Aug 1843
LEBERT, Jean Baptiste Romain, age 53, designer
Colmar   Mulhausen   London

8:0687   17 Aug 1843
SITTER? (LITTER?), Jean, age 30, factory worker
Willer   Urbes   New York

8:0690   18 Aug 1843
MARX, Elisabeth, age 25
(none)   Pfaffenheim   Schefferson,
                                (Jefferson),
                                America

8:0691   18 Aug 1843
PETIT, Francois, age 22, factory worker
Cernay   Bitschwiller   New York

8:0702   23 Aug 1843
HAURY, Henry, age 42, calico printer
N? Merschwiller? N? Merschwiller   London

8:0710   25 Aug 1843
GUDELACH, Charles, age 22, chemist
Hesse Cassel,   Thann   London
    Hessen

8:0716   28 Aug 1843
HUGUOT?, Jean Pierre, age 38, landowner; with wife &
    2 children
Chavannes-le-   Chavannes-le- New York
Grand   Grand

8:0722   30 Aug 1843
PIERRON, Nicolas, age 73, carpenter
Dieuze?,   Ste.-Croix-   Hamburg
   Meurthe   a(ux)-M(ines)

8:0735   05 Sep 1843
WAPLER, Emile, age 23, businessman
Strasbourg   Mulhausen   New Orleans

8:0736   05 Sep 1843
CAYOT, Francois, age 44, farmer; with wife & 4 chil-
    dren
Renney?   Renney   New York
  (Benney?)

8:0759   16 Sep 1843
EHLINGER, Marie Anne, age 42, wife of (--) HRUB,
    dressmaker
Bitschwiller   Thann   Buffalo, America

8:0781   27 Sep 1843
BRAND, Catherine, age 54, wife of J(osep)h SCHUH
Burnhaupt-Haut   Burnhaupt-Haut Erie?, America

8:0783   29 Sep 1843
SCHMERBER? (SCHWERTER?), Morand, age 24, nailmaker?
Rixheim   Rixheim   San Antonio, Re-
                                public of Texas

8:0790   03 Oct 1843
SAUTER? (LAUTER?), Benoit?, age 62, daylaborer; with
    wife & 2? children
(none)   Riedesheim?   Texas, America

8:0795   05 Oct 1843
IDOUX, Francois Joseph, age 46, farmer; with wife &
    2? children
Salmbach,   Mulhausen   Texas, America
  Bas-Rhin

8:0796   05 Oct 1843
QUALLIER? (QUALLIN?), Francois? (Ferdinand?), age
    52, mechanic; with Maurice
Jouy,   Cernay   Texas, America
  Seine-et-Oise

8:0798   06 Oct 1843
SCHATZ, Joseph, age 62, landowner; with wife & 5?
    children
(none)   Riedesheim   Texas, America

8:0801   10 Oct 1843
PFAULENDRE? (THAULENDRE?), --, age 35, coachman
Klaenthof?,   Mulhausen   New York
  Wuerttemberg

8:0802   13 Oct 1843
HOFFMEYER, Bernard, age 37, farmer; with wife & 6
    children
Rouffach   Rouffach   Jefferson, Amer-
                                         ica

8:0803   13 Oct 1843
SCHREIBER, Jean, age 31, mattress maker?
Westphallen   Westphallen   Jefferson, Amer-
  (Westphalia)   (Westphalia)   ica

8:0829   02 Nov 1843
WEILL, Regine, age 22
Wallwiller   Wallwiller   New Orleans

8:0831   03 Nov 1843
MARTIN, Madeleine, age 26, domestic
Lobsann?   Guebwiller   Guatemala

8:0833   07 Nov 1843
RINPEL?, Charles, age 21, commercial agent
Mulhausen   Mulhausen   New Orleans

8:0836   09 Nov 1843
WALLIS, Jules, age 13
Paris   Altkirch   New York

8:0844   15 Nov 1843
GHLES? (IHLER?), Martin, age 41, farmer; with 2
    nephews
Rouffach   Rouffach   Jefferson, Amer-
                                         ica

8:0845   15 Nov 1843
PROBST, J(osep)h?, age 31, farmer; with 7 --?
Rouffach   Rouffach   Jefferson, Amer-
                                         ica

8:0846   15 Nov 1843
VOGT, Pierre, age 32, farmer
Rouffach   Rouffach   Jefferson, Amer-
                                         ica

8:0847   15 Nov 1843
IHLER, Paul, age 40, farmer; with wife & 7? children
Rouffach   Rouffach   Jefferson, Amer-
                                         ica

8:0848   15 Nov 1843
PROBST, Jean, age 18, farmer
Rouffach   Rouffach   Jefferson, Amer-
                                         ica

8:0849   15 Nov 1843
SOMMEREISEN, Joseph, age 40, farmer; with wife & 2
    children
Rouffach   Rouffach   Jefferson, Amer-
                                         ica

8:0852   15 Nov 1843
FLECHT? (HECHT?), Joseph, age 24, carpenter
Rouffach   Rouffach   Jefferson, Amer-
                                         ica

8:0853   15 Nov 1843
KEMPF, Joseph, age 34, carpenter; with wife & 2?
    children
Meyenheim   Meyenheim   Texas

8:0857   21 Nov 1843
WAPLER, Frederic Guillaume, age 54, businessman
Strasbourg   Mulhausen   New Orleans

8:0865   24 Nov 1843
THUET, Joseph, age 25, locksmith
Gundolsheim   Gundolsheim   Texas

8:0873   28 Nov 1843
NEUMEYER, Martin, age 42, winegrower; with wife
    Marie SINGER & 2 children (Anne Marie NEUMEYER,
    age 9, & Martin, age 6)
Rouffach   Rouffach   Jefferson, USA

8:0874   28 Nov 1843
HALM, Dominique, age 38, farmer
Dornach   Dornach   New York

8:0876   29 Nov 1843
SIMCKER, Jean Jacques, age 38, locksmith; with wife
    & 2? children
Riguewihr?   Thann   Texas

8:0893   06 Dec 1843
REICH, Jacques, age 34, farmer
Liegue?   Mulhausen   Philadelphia
  (Siegue?)

8:0895   11 Dec 1843
MOSSER, Fidele, age 30, winegrower; with wife
Rouffach   Rouffach   · Jefferson, Amer-
                                   ica

8:0901   14 Dec 1843
PETER, Jean, age 37, butcher
Feldbach   Feldbach   New York

8:0902   18 Dec 1843
KOENIGSECKER, Romain Nicolas, age 27, tilemaker?
   --?; with wife & 2? children
Rouffach   Rouffach   Philadelphia

8:0903   18 Dec 1843
NOBLAT, Jean Pierre, age 20, --?
Velescot   Velescot   New York

8:0904   19 Dec 1843
BELAET, Joseph, age 20, workman?; with wife
Velescot   Velescot   New York

8:0916   29 Dec 1843
BLACHER, Octave, age 29, civil engineer
Argemin?,   Mulhausen? (or London
 Calvados   Argemin?)

8:0923   10 Jan 1844
GSELL, Louis, age 34, commercial traveler
Niederentzen?   Niederentzen?   Jefferson, Amer-
                                   ica

8:0927   10 Jan 1844
GRIME, Pierre, age 43, farmer; with wife & 5 chil-
   dren
Vellescot   Vellescot   New York

8:0930   15 Jan 1844
ROUECHE, Theophile, age 19, commercial traveler
Brebotte   Brebotte   New York

8:0931   15 Jan 1844
GUERRY, Jean Pierre, age 29, nailmaker?; with wife &
   1 child
Faverois   Faverois   New York

8:0945   20 Jan 1844
MULLER, Jean, age 39, farmer
Niederentzen   Niederentzen   Jefferson, Amer-
                                   ica

8:0950   25 Jan 1844
CHOPIUS? (CHOPINS?), Frederic, age 19
Croix   Croix   New York

8:0952   29 Jan 1844
SCHEIBLE, Jean, age 49, mechanic
Seckingen,   Soultz   Matamoros, Amer-
 Baden   ica

8:0956   30 Jan 1844
VERAIN, Henry, age 29, designer?; with mother?, --?
   & 1 servant
Vellescot   Vellescot   New York

8:0961   02 Feb 1844
MAILLARD, Marie, age 23
Bretagne   Bretagne   New York

8:0962   02 Feb 1844
BORON, Jean Pierre, age 34, farmer; with father-in-
   law, mother-in-law, wife, & 7? children
Bretagne   Bretagne   New York

8:0963   02 Feb 1844
MAILLARD, Antoine, age 28, farmer
Bretagne   Bretagne   New York

8:0966   02 Feb 1844
VALLAT? (VOLLAT?), Francois, age 26
Recouvrance?   Recouvrance?   New York

8:0969   02 Feb 1844
RETAIT? (BETAIT?), Francois, age 20
Turkheim   Bretagne   New York

8:0970   08 Feb 1844
LALLEMENT, Henri, age 47, farmer & carpenter; with
   wife & 3 children
Rornach?   Thann   New York
  (Bornach?)

8:0972   10 Feb 1844
MAILLARD, Henry, age 28
Bretagne   Bretagne   New York

8:0976   12 Feb 1844
SCHEIDECKER, Jean, age 26, farmer
Rornach   Rornach   New York

8:0978   13 Feb 1844
HENRI? (SCHEURI?), Francois, age 61, farmer; with
   son
Freme,   Boron   New York
  Haut-Saone

8:0980   14 Feb 1844
PEROT, Pierre, age 36, farmer; with wife
Brebotte   Brebotte   New York

8:0981   14 Feb 1844
VALLAT, Francois, age 49, farmer; with wife & 6
   children
Brebotte   Brebotte   New York

8:0982   14 Feb 1844
PARRET, Jean Baptiste, age 44, farmer
Tuix   Tuix   New York

8:0983   14 Feb 1844
JEAN PIERRE?, Marie Louise, age 26, domestic; with 1
   child
Seroance?,   Tuix? (or   New York
  Haut-Saone   Seroance?)

8:0984   14 Feb 1844
COLIN, Joseph, age 30, charcoal burner
Tuix   Tuix   New York

8:0988   15 Feb 1844
HUFER, Marie Catherine, age 38, seamstress?
Honbourg?   Guebwiller   New York
  (Horbourg?)

8:0990   17 Feb 1844
DROG? (BROG?), Marie Agnes, age 29
(none)   Chaux   New York

8:0992   17 Feb 1844
VERNI? (VERNE?), Dominique, age 23, brewery? cooper
Guebwiller   Guebwiller   New York

8:1007   24 Feb 1844
MARSOT, Francois, age 45, edge-tool maker
(none)   Tuix   New York

8:1009   27 Feb 1844
DIRRIG? (BIRRIY?), Louis Aloyse, age 19, laborer?
Leymen   Leymen   New York

8:1010   27 Feb 1844
DREYER, Jean, age 27, turner
Leymen   Leymen   New York

8:1013   28 Feb 1844
RAMESIN, Jacques, age 59, farmer
Eguenique?   Eguenigue?   Philadelphia
  (Equenigue?)   (Equenigue?)

8:1014   28 Feb 1844
HETZMANN? (KLETZMANN?), Francois, age 25, carpenter
Flosme   Montreux? Cha- New York
                teau

8:1019   04 Mar 1844
CHOFFAT? (GROFFAT?), Pierre Francois, age 31, farmer
Foussemagne   Foussemagne   New York

8:1024   08 Mar 1844
ROLL, Therese, age 36; with 1 child
(none)   Kiffis?   New York

8:1025   08 Mar 1844
STEHLIN, Martin, age 50, baker; with wife & 3 chil-
  dren
Altingen,   Mulhausen   New York
  Bas-Rhin

8:1027   09 Mar 1844
ROLL, Martin, age 40, shoemaker
(none)   Kiffis   New York

8:1029   09 Mar 1844
ROLL, Bernard, age 39, shoemaker
(none)   Kiffis   New York

8:1034   13 Mar 1844
FREYBURGER, Marie Anne, age 21, dressmaker
Brechaumont   Brechaumont   New York

8:1035   13 Mar 1844
CLOR, Jean Thiebaut, age 30, farmer
Brechaumont   Brechaumont   New York

8:1036   13 Mar 1844
BLONDE, Francois Joseph, age 35, farmer
Brechaumont   Brechaumont   New York

8:1044   16 Mar 1844
ENDERLIN, Thiebaut, age 27, baker
Sausheim?   Sausheim?   New York
  (Lausheim?)   (Lausheim?)

8:1045   18 Mar 1844
ESCHIENSCHANG?, Etienne, age 46, farmer; with wife &
    7? children
Roedersdorff   Roedersdorff   New York

8:1050   21 Mar 1844
BLONDE, Nicolas, age 25, farmer
Brechaumont   Brechaumont   New York

8:1052   21 Mar 1844
MUNSCH, Erasme, age 21, farmer
Kruth   Felleringen   New Orleans

8:1056   26 Mar 1844
COTTET, Francois Joseph, age 42, farmer; with wife &
    5 children
Bourogne   Bourogne   New York

8:1057   26 Mar 1844
TAICHEUR, Francois, age 44, farmer; with wife & 6
    children
Bourogne   Bourogne   New York

8:1058   26 Mar 1844
GUANE? (QUANE?), Joseph, age 32, carpenter; with
    wife & 3 children
Courtelevant?   Bourogne   New York
  (Countelevant?)

8:1059   26 Mar 1844
MERCIER, Dominique, age 42, farmer; with wife & 3
    children
Bourogne   Bourogne   New York

8:1060   26 Mar 1844
FLOTAT, Jean Pierre, age 34, farmer
Meroux   Meroux   New York

8:1061   27 Mar 1844
STAUFFER?, Charles --?, age 28, farmer
Morvillars?   Morvillars?   New York

8:1062   28 Mar 1844
GISSELBRECHT, Jean Michel, age 32, weaver
Baldenheim,   Ribeauville   Buffalo, America
  Bas-Rhin

8:1068   02 Apr 1844
ROTH, Pierre, age 34, farmer
Dambley,   Beaucourt,   New York
  Doubs   Haut-Rhin

8:1069   02 Apr 1844
MERCKLEN, Thiebaut Henri, age 49, wagoner
Thann   Thann   New York

8:1070   02 Apr 1844
ROTH, Christophe, age 36, farmer
Epincourt,   Beaucourt   New York
  Doubs

8:1071   02 Apr 1844
HAGENBACH, Meinrad, age 32, farmer; with wife, 2
   children, & sister-in-law
N. Morschwiller   Guebwiller   New Orleans

8:1072   02 Apr 1844
ZURCHER, Jean Georges, age 13
Mulhausen   Mulhausen   London

8:1075   03 Apr 1844
KAEUFFER, Jean Baptiste, age 27, carpenter?
Oberfrasheim?   Kuenheim?   New York
  (Oberfaasheim?)

8:1076   04 Apr 1844
STRUDEL? (STRADEL?), Charles?, age 29, wheelwright
Itthaeuseren?   Guemar   New York

8:1078   04 Apr 1844
DONZE, Pierre Francois, age 34, locksmith
Beaucourt   Beaucourt   New York

8:1090   12 Apr 1844
ROTH, Chretien, age 24, profession not given
Bollwiller   Bellemagny   New York

8:1092   13 Apr 1844
CLUERR? (AUERR?), Jean, age 30, cooper & brewer?
Felleringen   Felleringen   New York

8:1100   17 Apr 1844
WEINMANN, Jean, age 23, domestic
Gimmersdorff   Gimmersdorff   New York

8:1118   23 Apr 1844
JUILLARD, Nicolas, age 46, weaver; with wife & 5
   children
Ostheim   Ostheim   New York

8:1119   23 Apr 1844
MONSCHEIN, Michel, age 33, joiner; with wife & 2
   children
Ostheim   Ostheim   New York

8:1120   23 Apr 1844
COMMERY?, Jean, the younger, age 46, carpenter; with
   wife, 4 children, & has father
Ostheim   Ostheim   New York

8:1121   23 Apr 1844
RIEGERT, Nicolas, age 43, farmer; with wife & 8
   children
Hombourg   Hombourg   New York

8:1123   23 Apr 1844
RICHARD, Henri, age 30, profession not given
--   Faverois   New York

8:1124   24 Apr 1844
STAMM? (STRAMM?, HAMM?), Samuel, age 36, builder &
   machinist
Cranieremont?,   Thann,   London
  Vosges   Haut-Rhin

8:1154   07 May 1844
CLAIROTET? (CLAIROLET?), Dominique Constant, age
   35?, profession illegible
Neuf Brisach   Cernay   Texas

8:1156   07 May 1844
VEY, Joseph, age 28, property owner; with wife & 2?
   children
Soppe-Le-Haut   Soppe-Le-Haut   New York

8:1165   11 May 1844
SPECHT, Valentin, age 24, cloth printer
Husseren?   Husseren?   New Orleans

8:1166   11 May 1844
PANTALEON, Simon, age 23, cloth printer
Mollau?   Felleringen   New York

8:1169   14 May 1844
IMBER, Georges, age 51, carpenter
Mulhausen   Wolschwiller   New York

8:1174   15 May 1844
LUTHRINGER, Balthazar, age 24, cloth printer
Mitzach   Mitzach   New York

8:1195   27 May 1844
URBAN, Jean Georges, age 45, handworker
Guebwiller   Guebwiller   New York

8:1210   06 Jun 1844
SCHAGENE? (SCHAGINE?), Joseph, age 30, daylaborer;
   with wife & 2 children
Soppe-le-Haut   Soppe-le-Haut   New York

8:1245   24 Jun 1844
ROESCHARD?, Jean Georges, age 35, gardener; with
   wife & 1 child
Weil, Baden   Mulhausen   Philadelphia

8:1257   29 Jun 1844
MAST? (MUST?), Nicolas, age 17, handworker
Ranspach?   Thann   Augusta, North
                                          America

8:1267   04 Jul 1844
AMSTUTZ, Joseph, age 25, farmer
Leymen   Grandwillars   New York

8:1284   12 Jul 1844
BRUNSCHWICK, Cecile, age 26, no profession
Belfort   Belfort   New Orleans

8:1287   16 Jul 1844
DIDIER, Jean Baptiste, age 30, shoemaker; with wife
   & 1 child
Courtegeny?   Beaucourt   Philadelphia
   (Courtegenez?),
   Switzerland

8:1293   20 Jul 1844
SCHULTZ, Pierre, age 56, property owner? & mechanic?
Huningen?   Huningen   London

8:1294   20 Jul 1844
CHIAPPINI, Marie Jean Antoine, age 21, painter
St. Louis   St. Louis   London

8:1304   26 Jul 1844
NOTH, Jean Baptiste, age 22, lithographer
Mulhausen   Mulhausen   London

8:1311   30 Jul 1844
HALLER, Fortune Aloyse, age 22, tailor
Felleringen   Felleringen   New Orleans

8:1315   01 Aug 1844
BOUEDER?, Joseph, age 18, no profession
St. Amarin   St. Amarin   New York

8:1325   05 Aug 1844
GLADIEUX, Jean Pierre, age 34, farmer; with wife & 2
   children
Vellescot   Vellescot   New York

8:1326   05 Aug 1844
REISEL, Joseph, age 35, weaver; with wife & 2 chil-
   dren
Chavannes-le-   Boron   New York
   Grand

8:1330   07 Aug 1844
SARGER, Joseph, age 36, carter
Felleringen   Felleringen   New York

8:1331   07 Aug 1844
SCHMITT, Madelaine, age 25, carter
Felleringen   Felleringen   New York

8:1332   07 Aug 1844
SARGER, Nicolas, age 33, saddler
Felleringen   Felleringen   New York

8:1336   08 Aug 1844
WELCKER, Hubert, age 18, salesman
Ranspach   Ranspach   New York

8:1344   12 Aug 1844
THUNBERG? (RUMBERG?), Antoine, age 23, tailor?
Delle   Vellescot   New York

8:1348   14 Aug 1844
CONRAD, Zacharie, age 25, factory laborer
Felleringen   Felleringen   New York

8:1351   16 Aug 1844
HEIDET, Francois Xavier, age 24, farmer; with Joseph
   LAURENT
Felon? (Telon?) Felon? (Telon?) New York

8:1356   19 Aug 1844
DARDEL, Claude, age 45, designer
Lyon   Mulhausen?   London

8:1372   24 Aug 1844
FELDER, Francois Joseph, age 45, metal turner; with
   wife, 6 children, & father
St. Amarin   St. Amarin   New York

8:1376   27 Aug 1844
SCHERTEN, Michel, age 22, tailor
Felleringen   Felleringen   New York

8:1377   27 Aug 1844
SCHERLEN, Pierre, age 20, tailor
Felleringen   Felleringen   New York

8:1378   27 Aug 1844
BOBENRIETH, Rene, age 19, engraver
Felleringen   Felleringen   New York

8:1379   27 Aug 1844
BINDER, Joseph, age 19, factory worker
Felleringen   Felleringen   New York

8:1380   27 Aug 1844
BINDER, Joseph*, age 18, daylaborer
Felleringen   Felleringen   New York
* So given.

8:1382   28 Aug 1844
MULLER, Antoine, age 36, turner?
Kaysersberg   Kaysersberg   New Orleans

8:1384   28 Aug 1844
GULLY, Max? (Mar?)-minicus?, age 49, joiner; with
   wife & 2 children
Ranspach   Ranspach   New York

8:1386   28 Aug 1844
SCHMITT, Nicolas, age 40, carter; with wife & 6
   children
Ranspach   Ranspach   New York

8:1387   28 Aug 1844
NAGLER, Henry, age 20, baker
Ranspach   Ranspach   New York

8:1388   28 Aug 1844
KESSLER, Augustin, age 30, turner; with wife & 1?
   child
Ranspach   Ranspach   New York

8:1389   28 Aug 1844
SIMON, Francois Antoine, age 40, baker
Mollau?   Ranspach   New York

8:1390   28 Aug 1844
KESSLER, Jean, son of Gaspard (KESSLER?), age 49?,
   factory worker; with wife & 1? child
Ranspach   Ranspach   New York

8:1391   28 Aug 1844
KURTZMANN, Jean, age 25, factory worker
Moosch   Moosch   New Orleans

8:1392   28 Aug 1844
PETER, Francois Antoine, age 30, factory worker
Moosch   Moosch   New Orleans

8:1393   28 Aug 1844
BUETIGER? (BIETIGER?), Jean, age 26? (36?), day-
   laborer; with wife & 5 children
--   Folkwiller?   New Orleans
                   (Falkwiller?)

8:1398   30 Aug 1844
WAPLER, Emile, age 24, businessman
Strasbourg   Mulhausen   New Orleans

8:1400   31 Aug 1844
KELLER, Gustave, age 29, farmer; with wife, 3 chil-
   dren, & mother-in-law
Chaux   Boron   New Orleans

8:1402   31 Aug 1844
SINGER, Jean Pierre, age 67, vine-dresser; with wife
   & 1? child
Soultzbach   Rouffach   Jefferson, Amer-
                                   ica

8:1404   03 Sep 1844
BARDOT, Pierre Francois, age 21, farmer
Lachapelle-   Lachapelle-   New York
   Sous-Chaux   Sous-Chaux

8:1405   03 Sep 1844
BARDOT, Jean Claude, age 23, farmer
Lachapelle-   Lachapelle-   New York
   Sous-Chaux   Sous-Chaux

8:1406   04 Sep 1844
DETAIT, Henri, age 51, farmer; with wife & 2 chil-
   dren
Vellescot   Vellescot   New York

8:1407   04 Sep 1844
FRICKER, Pierre, age 48, landowner; with wife
Soppe-le-Haut   Soppe-le-Haut   New York

8:1408   05 Sep 1844
DIETRICH, Bernard, age 21, baker
Turckheim   Mulhausen   New York

8:1409   05 Sep 1844
CHOFFAT, Catharine, widow? of ROSSI, age 37, baker;
   with 3 children
Bretagne   Bretagne   New York

8:1410   05 Sep 1844
SCHWARTZ, Joseph Francois, age 22, baker
Grosne?   Grosne?   New Orleans

8:1411   05 Sep 1844
TSCHIRHART, Nicolas, age 30, landowner
Soppe-le-Haut   Soppe-le-Haut   New York

8:1416   07 Sep 1844
ROHLINGER, Georges, age 42, mechanic; with wife
Deux Ponts,   Mulhausen?   New York
   Bavaria (Zwei-
   bruecken)

8:1420   07 Sep 1844
DESPREY? (BESPREY?), Xavier, age 37?, farmer; with
   wife & 1 child
Bretagne   Bretagne   New York

8:1421   10 Sep 1844
SALCHRATH, Joseph, age 41, handworker; with wife & 1
   child
Guebwiller   Guebwiller   Jefferson, USA

8:1422   10 Sep 1844
LORENTZ, Francois Joseph, age 34, weaver
Sentheim   Sentheim   New Orleans

8:1423   10 Sep 1844
GALLAT, Xavier, age 32, baker
Sentheim   Sentheim   New Orleans

8:1427   10 Sep 1844
MULLER, Francois Joseph, age 26, farmer
Falkviller   Falkviller   New Orleans

8:1432   13 Sep 1844
PREVOST, Pierre, age 49?, mechanic; with wife & 2
   children
Lixheim,   Cernay   St. Louis, Amer-
   Meurthe   ica

8:1433   13 Sep 1844
WOLF, Benjamin, age 44, mechanic; with wife &
   child? (children?)
Esslingen,   Cernay?   St. Louis, Amer-
   Wuerttemberg   ica

8:1434   13 Sep 1844
PFANNER, Jean Gregoire, age 41, priest
Altkirch   Soppe-le-Bas   New Orleans

8:1443   17 Sep 1844
SCHWENDENMANN? (SCHWINDENMANN?), Andre, age 44, car-
   penter
--   Sentheim   New Orleans

8:1444   18 Sep 1844
LUTTENSCHLAGER, Leger, age 34, daylaborer
Sentheim   Sentheim   New Orleans

8:1446   18 Sep 1844
MARTIN, Simon, age 23, engraver; with wife
Ranspach   Husseren?   New Orleans

8:1450   19 Sep 1844
EICHER, Chretien, age 24, farmer
Bisel   Staffelden   New York

8:1453   20 Sep 1844
RIMDER? (REMDER?), Sebastien, age 40, farmer
Rixheim   Rixheim   New York

8:1455   20 Sep 1844
LEMAIRE, Dominique, age 28, metal turner
Texouin?   Mulhausen?   New York
  (Pexouin?),
  Meurthe

8:1458   21 Sep 1844
CORDONNIER, Nicolas, age 40, landowner
Bretten   Bretten   Philadelphia

8:1459   21 Sep 1844
REDERSDORFF, Jean, age 38, farmer; with wife & chil-
   dren
Kettlach   Kettlach   Kentor, Ohio

8:1461   21 Sep 1844
EHLINGER, Napoleon, age 34, wood engraver?
Storckensohn   Storckensohn   New York

8:1462   21 Sep 1844
GRUNEISEN, Joseph, age 58, farmer
Soppe-le-Bas   Soppe-le-Bas   Columbia, Amer-
                                        ica

8:1463   21 Sep 1844
SCHERRER, Jacques, age 33, shoemaker
Soppe-le-Bas   Soppe-le-Bas   Columbia, Amer-
                                        ica

8:1467   23 Sep 1844
MURA, Jean, age 19, cloth printer
Husseren   ... St. Amarin   New York

8:1468   23 Sep 1844
HAGENBACH? (HUGENBACH?), Marie Margarete, age 26,
   cloth printer; with Henriette ... RINNER?
Munster   Guebwiller   London

8:1470   24 Sep 1844
SCHNEIDER, Alexandre, age 20, cooper
Husseren,   Husseren,   New York
  St. Amarin   St. Amarin

8:1471   24 Sep 1844
STEHLIN, Aloyse, age 35, tailor
Ollingen   Ollingen   Cincinnati

8:1474   25 Sep 1844
REBRASSIE, Marie, age 50, chemist
--   Bretagne   New York

8:1480   28 Sep 1844
GULLY, Alexandre, age 38, designer
Mollau?   Husseren   New York

8:1482   28 Sep 1844
SCHILLING, Charles, age 29, engraver
Felleringen   Husseren,   New York
                   Arond(issement)
                   Belfort

8:1486   03 Oct 1844
RINKER, Jean Jacques, age 46, carpenter
Hertmanns-   Mulhausen?   New York
  weiler?,
  Wuerttemberg

8:1489   03 Oct 1844
STUCKER, Georges, age 20, -- turner
Rammersmatt   Rammersmatt   New York

8:1490   03 Oct 1844
SCHENECKER?, Jean, age 22, weaver
Brechaumont   Brechaumont   New Orleans

8:1492   05 Oct 1844
HAUSER, Jean Adam, age 45, former registrar
--   Altkirch   London

8:1496   08 Oct 1844
MEYER, Joseph, age 39, cooper; with wife & 6? chil-
   dren
Bourbach-le-Bas Bourbach-le-Bas   New York

8:1497   08 Oct 1844
BILHARTZ, Joseph, age 44, baker
Feuersheim?   Soppe-le-Bas   Philadelphia
  (Faversheim?)
  Bas-Rhin

8:1498   08 Oct 1844
TREFF? (TRIFF?), Jacques, age 33, daylaborer
Soppe-le-Bas   Soppe-le-Bas   Columbia, Amer-
                                        ica

8:1499   08 Oct 1844
MENNINGER?, Francois Joseph, age 28, baker
Baldersheim   Baldersheim   Cincinnati

8:1500   08 Oct 1844
ZINCK, Francois Joseph, age 57, shoemaker; with
    wife? & children
Wittenheim   Sunsheim?   Cincinnati

8:1501   08 Oct 1844
STEHLIN, Antoine, age 46, tailor
Oltingen   Oltingen?   Cincinnati

8:1502   08 Oct 1844
GEBER, Joseph, age 38, nailmaker
Altkirch   Altkirch   New York

8:1505   09 Oct 1844
RUNDER, Benoit, age 35, printer on paper; with wife
    & 3 children
Rixheim   Rixheim   New York

8:1506   09 Oct 1844
GASSER, Francois Joseph, age 28, daylaborer; with
    wife & 1 child
Niederhugenthal Niederhugenthal New York

8:1510   10 Oct 1844
VERNETTE, Louis, age 28, farmer; with wife?, child,
    & sister-in-law
Bretten   Bretten   New Orleans

8:1511   10 Oct 1844
SITTRE? (LITTRE?), Joseph, age 38, farmer; with wife
    & 3 children
Bretten   Bretten   New Orleans

8:1512   10 Oct 1844
TINGENOT, Jean Nicolas, age 45, farmer
Bretten   Bretten   New Orleans

8:1513   10 Oct 1844
TINGUEOT, Pierre Francois, age 34, farmer; with wife
Bretten   --   New Orleans

8:1517   10 Oct 1844
BRADHAG?, Joseph, age 34, parish baker; with wife
Blodelsheim   Mulhausen?   New Orleans

8:1520   12 Oct 1844
DORNOUGE?, Pierre, age 31, farmer
Angeot?   Angeot?   Columbus, Amer-
                                      ica

8:1524   15 Oct 1844
CORDONNIER, Nicolas, age 32, profession not given
Bretten   Lachapelle-   New Orleans
                   sous-Rougemont

8:1525   15 Oct 1844
TAUTSCH, Francois Eugene, age 14, farmer
Rougemont   (La)chapelle-   New Orleans
                   sous-Rougemont

8:1526   15 Oct 1844
HALLER, Francois Richard, age 29, joiner; with wife
    & 1 child
Felleringen   Felleringen   New Orleans

8:1527   15 Oct 1844
TSCHAUN?, Jean, age 56, daylaborer; with wife & 4
    children
Soppe-le-Bas   Soppe-le-Bas   Columbia, Amer-
                                      ica

8:1528   15 Oct 1844
CORDIER, Jean Baptiste, age 40, farmer
Bretten   Bretten   Philadelphia

8:1531   17 Oct 1844
RIEDEN, Jean, age 45, landowner; with wife & 2 chil-
    dren
Zillisheim   Zillisheim   Columbia, Amer-
                                      ica

8:1539   19 Oct 1844
DELARUE, Christoph, age 51, mechanic
Werentzhausen   Mulhausen   Virginia, Amer-
                                      ica

8:1547   21 Oct 1844
LENTZ, Joseph, age 16, daylaborer
Ueberkeimen?   Brechaumont   New Orleans

8:1548   21 Oct 1844
FRITZ, Louis, age 42, carpenter
Bretten   Bretten   Philadelphia

8:1549   21 Oct 1844
WILHELM, Joseph, age 24, farrier
Oderen?   Oderen?   New Orleans

8:1550   21 Oct 1844
SCHLOSSER, Pierre, age 38, weaver; with wife & 5
    children
Bourbach-le-Bas   Bourbach-le-Bas   New York

8:1552   22 Oct 1844
MONTAVON, Sebastien, age 54, farmer; with wife & 4
    children, & son-in-law
Rougemont   Rougemont   Philadelphia

8:1557   25 Oct 1844
WEIXLER?, Ursule, age 29, profession not given; with
    child
Leutkirch,   Mulhausen?   New Orleans
    Wuerttemberg

8:1566   31 Oct 1844
CALMELAT, Jacques, age not given, farmer; with wife
    & 2 children
Bretten   Bretten   Philadelphia

8:1567   31 Oct 1844
WASSEN, Antoine, age 39, shoemaker; with wife & 3
    children
Bourbach-le-Bas   Sentheim   New Orleans

8:1568   31 Oct 1844
BAUMGARTNER, Renaud, age 44, shoemaker
Massevaux   Sentheim?   New Orleans

8:1569   31 Oct 1844
REITZER, Ambroise, age 40, profession illegible;
    with wife & 3 children
Niederbruck?   Massevoux?   Philadelphia

8:1570   31 Oct 1844
ORIEZ, Pierre, age 44, farmer; with wife & 3 chil-
    dren
--   Lachapelle-   New York
                sous-Chaux

8:1572   04 Nov 1844
DE NEUVILLE, Albert Francois? Joseph, age 39, person
    of property
Fribourg (Frei-   Colmar   London
    burg), Grand
    Duchy of Baden

8:1577   04 Nov 1844
ENDERLIN, Henry, age 43, maker of cylinders; with
    wife
Courtavon?   Mulhausen?   New Orleans

8:1579   04 Nov 1844
RIFF, Xavier, age 37, daylaborer; with wife? & chil-
    dren
Soppe-le-Haut   Soppe-le-Haut   New Orleans

8:1581   05 Nov 1844
GIRARDEZ? (GIRARDEY?), Joseph, age 25, farmer; with
    wife, child, mother-in-law, & sister-in-law
Rougemont   Rougemont   Philadelphia

8:1582   05 Nov 1844
GOLLY, Joseph, age 28, printer
Felleringen   Felleringen   New York

8:1583   05 Nov 1844
BOBENRIETH, Jean, age 26, printer
Felleringen   Felleringen   New York

8:1584   05 Nov 1844
WISSANG, Jean, age 28, printer
Felleringen   Felleringen   New York

8:1589   06 Nov 1844
BENGUEREL, Zelime Henry, age 32, joiner
La-Chaux-de-   Mulhausen   New Orleans
    Fonds, Switzer-
    land

8:1590   06 Nov 1844
ORIEZ, Alexis, age 35, farmer; with wife & child
Chaux   Chaux   Philadelphia

8:1592   06 Nov 1844
PONDRE? (TONDRE?), Nicolas, age 42, farmer; with
    wife & 4 children
Bretten   Bretten   Philadelphia

8:1594   09 Nov 1844
FUCHS, Jacques, age 41, farmer; with 2 children &
    niece
Cernay   Cernay   New York

8:1595   09 Nov 1844
MUELLER, Francois Joseph, age 42, maker of --? --?;
    with wife & children
Turckheim   Wintzenheim   New Orleans

8:1597   11 Nov 1844
MEYER, Joseph, age 44, joiner; with wife & 7 chil-
    dren
Wittelsheim   Wittelsheim   New Orleans

8:1600   12 Nov 1844
STROHMEYER, Francois Joseph, age 52, farmer; with
    wife & 7 children
Burnhaupt-le-   Burnhaupt-le-   New York
    Haut   Haut

8:1606   13 Nov 1844
SCHNEBELIN, Barthelemi, age 20, baker
Bautzenheim   Hombourg   New Orleans

8:1608   13 Nov 1844
SCHOLL? (SCHOTT?), Antoine, age 68, profession not
    given; with daughter & 2 children
--   Wittelsheim   Texas

8:1609   13 Nov 1844
GAUCHEL, Francois, age 46, shoemaker; with daughter?
Belfort   Bretten   Philadelphia

8:1610   13 Nov 1844
MULLER, Michel, age 30, shoemaker?
--   Wittelsheim   Texas

8:1611   13 Nov 1844
WERNETTE, Jean Baptiste, age 31, profession illeg-
    ible
--   Wittelsheim   Texas

8:1612   13 Nov 1844
LIEBER? (LEIBER?), Dominique,   age 27, daylaborer;
   with wife
Wittelsheim   Wittelsheim   Texas

8:1615   14 Nov 1844
MENCHEZ?, Jean Claude, age 20, daylaborer?
Magny   Faverois   New York

8:1616   14 Nov 1844
DIETEMANN, Jean, age 34, farmer
Traubach-le-Haut Traubach-le-Haut   New Orleans

8:1617   14 Nov 1844
BETZINGER, Jean Jacques, age 33, weaver
Traubach-le-Haut Traubach-le-Haut   New Orleans

8:1620   14 Nov 1844
ABT, Laurent, age 28, vine-dresser
Riedisheim   Riedisheim   New Orleans

8:1623   18 Nov 1844
HACHLER? (KACHLER?), Catherine, age 24, baker
Guewenheim?   Soppe-le-Bas   Philadelphia

8:1628   19 Nov 1844
MEYER, Joseph, age 42, vine-dresser; with wife & 3
   children
Turckheim   Turckheim   New Orleans

8:1631   21 Nov 1844
CHARBONNIER, Antoine Amedee, age 40, civil engineer
Laon, Aisne   Mulhausen?   London

8:1632   22 Nov 1844
TACGUARD, Jacques, age 40?, daylaborer; with wife &
   3 children
Vauthiermont   Vauthiermont   New York

8:1665   06 Dec 1844
DESPREZ? (DESPREY?), Andre Celestin, age 20, joiner
Grosne   Vezelois   New York

8:1668   06 Dec 1844
SCHMEIBER? (SCHMABER?), Elisabeth, age 43, factory
   worker; with 1 child
Mulhausen   Thann   New Orleans

8:1669   07 Dec 1844
LOEFFEL, Appolinaire, age 42, weaver?
Vieux-Thann   Felleringen   New York

8:1675   14 Dec 1844
JODRE? (JODIE?), Michel, age 19, farmer
Grandvillars   Spechbach-le-   Ohio, America
                  Haut

8:1676   16 Dec 1844
MEISE? (MEISI?), Agathe, age 33, factory worker
Blotzheim   Thann   New Orleans

8:1679   21 Dec 1844
HEISLEN, Laurent, age 29, locksmith; with brother
Rouffach   Rouffach   Jefferson, Amer-
                                     ica

8:1682   30 Dec 1844
SCHERTZ, Charles, age 28, musician
Riedisheim   Riedisheim   New Orleans

Jacquemin, 7:1432

Jacquot, 7:0835

Jaeglen, 7:1548

Jaegy, 7:1425

Jean-Pierre, 8:0983

Jeannez, 7:0838

Jehlen, 7:0359

Jeisch, 7:16289

Jelsch, 7:2623

Jobert, 7:1486, 7:2156, 8:0669

Joder, 7:2052, 7:2498, 7:2499

Jodie (Jodre), 8:1675

Johvettel, 7:2312

Juen(n), 7:0282, 7:2684

Juillard, 8:1118

Jullerad, 7:1012

Jung, 7:2027

Kachler, 8:1623

Kaeuffer, 8:1075

Karrer, 7:0375

Kauffmann, 7:0300, 7:0301

Keiflin, 7:1270

Keller, 8:1400

Kellermann, 7:1677

Kempf, 7:1426, 8:0853

Kessler, 7:1272, 8:1388, 8:1390

Kircher, 7:0913

Kirscher, 7:0957, 7:1464, 7:1489, 7:1490

Klein, 7:1182

Kleinfeld, 7:0934

Kletzmann, 8:1014

Klopfenstein, 7:2110

Klopfstein, 7:1137

Knoll, 7:0550

Koch, 7:0602, 7:0849, 7:0921, 7:1365, 7:1989

Kochlin, 7:2288

Koechin, 7:1363

Koechlin, 7:0904

Koenig, 8:0107

Koenigsecker, 8:0902

Koince, 7:0594

Krafft, 8:0473

Kreybull, 7:0819, 7:0820

Kreyenbuhl, 7:2656

Kreyer, 7:0739

Kreyscher, 7:2000

Kropf, 7:2184

Krust, 7:1750

Kuenemann, 7:1361

Kuentz, 7:2131

Kuppelmeyer, 7:1535

Kurtzmann, 8:1391

Kuttler, 7:1419

Lagresse (Laguesse), 7:0573

Lallement, 8:0970

Lambelin, 7:1353

Langard, 7:1330

Langenfeld, 7:0771

Lasche, 7:2064

Lassiat, 7:0555

Lauguard, 7:1330

Laurent, 8:1351

Lauter, 8:0790

Lebert, 7:2028, 8:0680

Leclaire, 8:0288

Lefebvre, 7:2291

Lehmes, 7:1265

Leiber, 8:1612

Lemaire, 8:1455

Lenlart, 7:1435

Lentz, 8:1547

Leromain, 7:0895
Levy, Introduction
Lichty, 7:2011

Lieber, 8:1612

Linsenboltz, 7:1455

Lischer, 7:2107

Litter, 8:0687

Littre, 8:1511

Loeffel, 8:1669

Lorentz, 7:1420, 8:1422

Lury, 7:2410

Luthringer, 8:1174

Lutigue, 7:0829

Lutringer, 7:1520

Luttenbacher, 7:0845

Luttenschlager, 8:1444

Maechler, 7:2693

Maillard, 8:0961, 8:0963, 8:0972

Maller, 7:1843

Maller. See also Miller, Mueller, Muller

Mansbendel, 7:0901

Marchal, 7:2111

Marchand, 7:0774

Marsot, 7:1497, 8:0455, 8:1007

Martin, 7:1160, 8:0831, 8:1446

Marx, 8:0690

Massey, 7:1841

Masson, 7:0871

Mast, 8:1257

Mattler, 8:0458

Maudrin, 7:0315

Meise (Meisi), 8:1676

Menchez, 8:1615

Menetre, 7:0834

Menninger, 8:1499

Mercier, 8:1059

Merciole, 7:0551

Mercklen, 8:1069

Mermot, 7:2261

Meyer, 7:0116, 7:0140, 8:1496, 8:1597, 8:1628

Migeon, 7:0643

Miller, 7:1313

Miller. See also Maller, Mueller, Muller

Minetrez, 7:1400

Moinet, 7:0279

Molly, 7:2510

Mondrux, 7:2442

Monnier, 7:1380, 7:2136

Monschein, 8:1119

Montavon, 8:1552

Moser, 8:0431

Mosser, 8:0895

Moulin, 7:1351, 7:1356

Moureaux, 7:1430

Mueller, 8:0613, 8:1595

Mueller. See also Maller, Miller, Muller

Mueth, 7:2636

Muller, 7:1475, 7:1516, 7:1843, 8:0499, 8:0945, 8:1382, 8:1427, 8:1610

Muller. See also Maller, Miller, Mueller

Munsch, 7:1299, 8:1052

34

Mura, 8:1467

Murbach, 7:2062

Murer (Mures), 7:1343

Must, 8:1257

Nachbaur, 8:0422

Nafzger, 7:2008

Nagler, 8:1387

Namze, 8:0139

Nasenforder, 7:1907

Neck, 7:0831

Neumeyer, 8:0873

Neuville, De, 8:1572

Niederhauser, 8:0676

Noblat, 8:0903

Norrot, 7:0433

Noth, 8:1304

Obdorff, 7:1433

Obrecht, 7:0789, 7:0805, 7:2579

Ochs, 7:0436

Oriez, 8:1570, 8:1590

Orlowsky, 7:1238

Orth, 7:1521

Ortscheidt, 7:1303

Osser, 7:1403

Pacguard, 8:1632

Pantaleon, 8:1166

Paquot, 7:0022

Parret, 8:0982

Peltier, 7:0275

Perot, 8:0980

Perrez, 7:1320

Peter, 8:0901, 8:1392

Petit, 7:2677, 8:0691

Petitjean, 7:1352

Pfanner, 8:1434

Pfaulendre, 8:0801

Pfeil, 7:0752

Pierre, 8:0983

Pierron, 8:0722

Pommier, 7:1329

Pondre, 8:1592

Pourche, 7:2125

Pourvourville, 7:1297

Praelke (Praetke), 7:1183

Prevost, 8:1432

Prevot, 7:1382

Probst, 8:0330, 8:0845, 8:0848

Pulcher, 7:1088, 8:0350

Py, 7:0061

Quallier (Quallin), 8:0796

Quane, 8:1058

Radelsperger, 7:2098

Ramesin, 8:1013

Rapine, 7:2519

Rebrassie, 8:1474

Redersdorff, 8:1459

Reich, 8:0893

Reich. See also Rich, Roesch, Roess, Roos, Roosz, Roueche, Rueche

Reinhard, 7:2535, 8:0435

Reis(s) 7:1147, 7:2312

Reisel, 8:1326

Reitzer, 8:1569

Remder, 8:1453

Renaud, 8:0665

Reset, 7:1334

Retait, 8:0969

Rich, 7:1852, 8:0480

Rich. See also Reich, Roesch, Roess, Roos, Roosz, Roueche, Rueche

Richard, 8:0418, 8:1123

Rick, 7:0801

Rieden, 8:1531

Riegert, 8:1121

Riff, 8:1579

Riffart, 7:1700

Rimbold, 7:1350

Rimder, 8:1453

Rinker, 8:1486

Rinner, 8:1468

Rinpel, 8:0833

Ripon, 7:1312

Risler, 7:1986, 8:0615

Rittner, 7:2266

Ritzenthaler, 7:0133

Rivez, 7:1388

Robay, 8:0104

Rock, 7:0828

Roesch, 7:0474, 7:2065

Roesch. See also Reich, Rich, Roess, Roos, Roosz, Roueche, Rueche

Roeschard, 8:1245

Roesle, 7:2065

Roess, 8:0453

Roess. See also Reich, Rich, Roesch, Roos, Roosz, Roueche, Rueche

Rohlinger, 8:1416

Roland, 7:1536

Roll, 8:1024, 8:1027, 8:1029

Roos, 7:0332, 7:0900

Roosz, 7:1499

Roos, Roosz. See also Reich, Rich, Roesch,

Roess, Roueche, Rueche

Rosselot, 7:0283, 7:0363

Rossi, 8:1409

Roth, 7:0013, 7:0768, 7:0793, 7:0795, 7:0796, 7:1281, 7:1283, 7:1563, 8:1068, 8:1070, 8:1090

Rothenburger, 7:1648

Rothmund, 7:2091

Roueche, 7:1037, 8:0930

Rueche, 7:1037, 7:1714

Roueche, Rueche. See also Reich, Rich, Roesch, Roess, Roos, Roosz

Rueter, 7:0994

Rumberg, 8:1344

Runder, 8:1505

Rupp, 7:1261, 7:0277

Ruyer, 7:0549

Salchrath, 8:1421

Sarger, 8:1330, 8:1332

Saussotte, 7:1422

Sauter, 8:0790

Sauvageot, 7:1151, 8:0596

Schacherer, 7:0479

Schaeffoldt, 8:0383

Schagene (Schagine), 8:1210

Schatz, 8:0798

Scheible, 8:0952

Scheidecker, 8:0976

Scheneberg, 8:0391

Schenecker, 8:1490

Scherlen, 8:1377

Scherrer, 8:1463

Scherten, 8:1376

EMIGRANTS FROM FRANCE (HAUT-RHIN DEPARTEMENT) TO AMERICA

PART 2: 1845-1847

Clifford Neal Smith

INTRODUCTION

This monograph continues a subseries (1837-1857) in which the emigrants from the Upper Alsace (Departement du Haut-Rhin) to the United States are set forth. Herein, will also be found the names of a number of emigrants from Germany and Switzerland who, although foreigners, apparently received passports from the French Haut-Rhin deparmental government.

The list of emigrants herein (1845-1847) has been extracted from registers 8 and 9 of passports issued by the departmental government for travel outside of France. Most of the entries in these registers record travel to European cities and, thus, are not of direct interest to American genealogical researchers. Only emigrants to the New World (Canada, Mexico, and the United States) are listed herein. The registers are to be found in the Archives Departmentales du Haut-Rhin in Colmar; they have been microfilmed by the Genealogical Society of Utah on microfilm roll 1,069,294.

The entries hereinafter are arranged in three lines:

First Line: Volume (registers 8 or 9) and entry number therein with the date of entry.

Second Line: Name of emigrant, age, and profession; accompanying family members.

Third Line: Probably, the place of birth or residence at time of emigration/probably the place of passport issuance, and destination as given to French authorities. (Since the register columns are not labeled, these places (birth, residence, and passport issuance) are only conjectural on the part of this compiler.)

The Surname Index begins at page 39 hereinafter.

8:1684   03 Jan 1845
KAUFMANN, Daniel, age 18, farmer
Bettendorf/ditto   Ohio, America

8:1688   06 Jan 1845
CHRISTEN, Joseph, age 20, printer
Felleringen/ditto   New York

8:1689   06 Jan 1845
HAUS? [HANS?], Gaspard, age 20, factory worker
Felleringen/ditto   New York

8:1692   07 Jan 1845
BOBENRIETH, Joseph, age 29, day laborer
Hussepen? [Husseren?]/ditto   New Orleans

8:1696   08 Jan 1845
HENZEL, Conrad Auguste, age 32, woodturner, with wife
    & children
Thann/ditto   New York

8:1703   15 Jan 1845
SCHUCHOLL? [SCHACHOLT?], Jean Baptiste, age 38
Ribeauville/ditto   New York

8:1708   24 Jan 1845
JACOB, Henri, age 31
Kruth/ditto   New York

8:1709   24 Jan 1845
FLIELLER? [FLIDLER?], Joseph, age 33, weaver
Kruth/ditto   New York

8:1712   25 Jan 1845
MUTH, Jacques, age 21, farmer
Seppois-le-Bois/ditto   Philadelphia

8:1714   25 Jan 1845
KAUFMANN, Joseph, age 21, farmer
Levoncourt?/Bettendorff

8:1716   28 Jan 1845
RESWEBER, Antoine, age 24, gardener
Roppentzwiller/Rexheim   Philadelphia

8:1718   29 Jan 1845
GROSS, Joseph, age 58, mason, with wife
Dieffenmatten/Soppe-le-Bas   New York

8:1724   03 Feb 1845
NASS, Augustin, age 35, butcher
Berrwiller/ditto   New Orleans

8:1727   05 Feb 1845
CLOR, Jean Baptiste, age 27, shoemaker, with wife
Brechaumont/ditto   Ohio

8:1728   05 Feb 1845
BURLIAT? Xavier, age 44, carpenter; with wife & 4
    children
Brechaumont/ditto   New York

8:1734   05 Feb 1845
SCHMIDT, Joseph, age 41, --?; with wife & 1 child
--/Sternenberg [Switzerland]   New York

8:1736   05 Feb 1845
BLEYER, Jean, age 60, day laborer; with wife & 5
    children
Dieffmatten [Switzerland]/ditto   New York

8:1738   12 Feb 1845
BIHL, Jean?, age 27, farmer
Traubach-le-Haut/Brechaumont   New York

8:1739   12 Feb 1845
MAILLARD, Louis, age 50, farmer; with wife & --?
Bretagne/ditto   New York

8:1740   12 Feb 1845
EICHINGER, Joseph, age 30, farmer; with wife & 1
    daughter
Traubach-le-Haut/ditto   Canada

8:1741   14 Feb 1845
GRISEZ, Nicolas, age 22, farmer
Lachapelle-sous-Chaux/ditto   New York

8:1742   13 Feb 1845
CHAPUIS, Pierre Julien, age 38, farmer
Lachapelle-sous-Chaux/ditto   New York

8:1748   17 Feb 1845
REPERT, Jacques Francois, age 31, tailor?
Chaux/ditto   New Orleans

8:1750   20 Feb 1845
BURLIAT, Jaques, age 30, day laborer; with wife &
    4 children
Brechaumont/ditto   New York

8:1751   20 Feb 1845
MAILLARD, Jean Pierre, age 41, farmer; with wife,
    mother-in-law, 2 children, & 1 domestic
--/Bretagne   New York

8:1752   20 Feb 1845
BLEYER, Sebastien, age 63, day laborer; with wife
Dieffmatten [Switzerland]/ditto   New York

8:1753   20 Feb 1845
MASSOT, Joseph, age 24, farmer
Chaux/ditto   New Orleans

1

2

8:1754   20 Feb 1845
GLADIEUX? [HADIEUX?], Philippe, age 58?, landowner
Vellescot/ditto   New York

8:1756   21 Feb 1845
CHAPUIS, Jean Baptiste Leonard, age 43, wheelwright;
   with wife & 3 children
--/Lachapelle-sous-Chaux   New York

8:1761   25 Feb 1845
TECKRE? Nicolas, age 44, farmer; with wife & 3 chil-
   dren
--/Chavannes-les-Grand   New York

8:1762   26 Feb 1845
FREY, Jean Thiebaud, age 38, farmer; with wife & 4
   children
Traubach-le-Bas/ditto   Canada

8:1763   26 Feb 1845
BURY, Jean, age 23, joiner
Gildwiller/Lauw   Canada

8:1765   28 Feb 1845
FREYBOURGER, Ignace, age 23, farmer
Traubach-le-Haut/ditto   Canada

8:1768   03 Mar 1845
HECK Madelaine, wife? of Ladan? MASSEY, age 3?, with
   children
Thann/ditto   Lower Sandusky, America

8:1769   03 Mar 1845
DANIEL, Marie Rosalie, age 21, domestic
Audincourt, Doubs/ditto   New York

8:1773   05 Mar 1845
GASSER, Anne Marie, age 29, waiting woman
Sierentz?/ditto   New York

8:1776   08 Feb 1845
SCHERNER, Madeleine, age 31?, day laborer
Traubach-le-Haut/ditto   New York

8:1780   11 Feb 1845
JENN, Marie Agathe, widow of GROB? [GROSS?], Martin,
   seamstress
Molleur?/ditto   Ohio

8:1783   14 Mar 1845
DRUY? [DREY?], Antoine, age 48, farmer; with wife &
   6 children
Durrenentzen/ditto   Chicago

8:1785   17 Mar 1845
SIGRIST, Jean Michel, age 31, --?
Beblenheim/Guebwiller   New York

8:1787   17 Mar 1845
VIENOT, Jacques, age 38, baker; with wife & 2 chil-
dren
Roche-les-Clamont?, Doubs/Muhlhausen   St. Louis,
                                          America

8:1788   17 Mar 1845
BARBARAS, Jacques, age 47, day laborer; with wife &
   2 children
Ostheim/ditto   New York

8:1789   17 Mar 1845
LINCK, Jacques, age 50, day laborer; with wife & 2
   children
Ostheim/ditto   New York

8:1790   17 Mar 1845
WEBER, Nicolas, age 56, farmer; with wife & 7 chil-
   dren
Ostheim/ditto   New York

8:1791   17 Mar 1845
PFUESTER? [PFIESTER?], Joseph, age 63, farmer; with
   wife & 6 children
Ostheim/ditto   New York

8:1792   17 Mar 1845
WICKERSHEIM, Frederic, age 35, weaver; with wife &
   5 children
Ostheim/ditto   New York

8:1793   17 Mar 1845
SCHNAEBELE, Jacques, age 60, farmer; with wife & 4?
   children
Baldenheim, Bas-Rhin/ditto   New York

8:1794   17 Mar 1845
LIECHLE, Pierre, age 44, [profession not given]
Bettendorff/Schlierbach   N--chling?, T--? America

8:1795   17 Mar 1845
MARCONNET, Suzanne Elisabeth, wife of -- KRAMCK? or
   KRANICK; with children
--/Thann   New York

8:1799   18 Mar 1845
JODER, Jean, age 49, day laborer; with 3 children
Steinbach/Walheim   New York

8:1800   18 Mar 1845
STUCKLE? Jean, age 46, farmer; with wife & 2 children
Feldbach/Schlierbach   N--chling?, T--? America

8:1805   19 Mar 1845
TRESCH, Madelaine, widow of -- CLER?, age 33; with
   3 children & sister?
Hericourt, Haute-Saone/Thann   New York

8:1808   21 Mar 1845
GEIL, Georges, age 28, farmer
Ostheim/ditto   New York

8:1809   21 Mar 1845
MEYER, N--?, age 27, farmer
Ostheim/ditto   New York

8:1810   21 Mar 1845
MEYER, Jean, age 29, sugar baker?
Ostheim/ditto   New York

8:1811   21 Mar 1845
HEMMERLE, Michel, age 26½, locksmith
Rouffach/ditto   Jefferson, America

8:1812   21 Mar 1845
CRITZ, Anne Eve, age 22, dressmaker
Guevenatten/Angeot   Gibarrez? Libanez? America

8:1814   25 Mar 1845
COUNNERY? Jean, age 19, carpenter
Ostheim/ditto   New York

8:1815   25 Mar 1845
NUDELHOFFER, Jean, age 27, joiner; with wife Guilla-
   min?
Ostheim/ditto   New York

8:1816   25 Mar 1845
HELD, Georges, age 25, tailor; with wife
Ostheim/ditto   New York

8:1817   26 Mar 1845
BRECHBUHLER, Isaac, age 48, day laborer; with wife &
   3 children
Ostheim/ditto   New York

8:1818   27 Mar 1845
KOHLER, Auguste, age 23, ecclesiastic attached to a
   foreign mission
Colmar/ditto   New Orleans

8:1824   01 Apr 1845
DIDIER, Francois, age 45, --?; with wife & 5 children
--/Mezire   New York

8:1828   02 Apr 1845
YARDOT? [YANDOT?], Jean Baptiste, age 36
Sermamagny/ditto   New York

8:1834   07 Apr 1845
UNGERER, Pierre, age 24, factory worker
Drachenbaum, Bas-Rhin/ Cernay   Amsterdamm, America

8:1835   07 Mar 1845
GALLIET, Jean Pierre, age 38, farmer; with wife &
   3 children
Bourogne/ditto   New York

8:1836   07 Mar 1845
CHABOUDE, Joseph, age 25, farmer; with wife & w chil-
   dren
Bourogne/ditto   New York

8:1837   07 Mar 1845
GRIESEMANN, Jean Pierre, age 43, farmer; with wife &
   4 children
Bourogne/ditto   New York

8:1838   08 Apr 1845
KASTLER, Michel, age 39, wine-grower; with wife &
   3 children
Ribeauville/ditto   New York

8:1845   09 Apr 1845
KIBLER, Jean Baptiste, age 22, --?
Geishausen?/ditto   New York

8:1846   09 Apr 1845
GULLY, Barnabe, age 28, --?
Geishausen?/ditto   New York

8:1847   09 Apr 1845
MUECHLER, Ignace, age 25, vinegrower; with wife &
   sister
Legolsheim?/Ribeauville   New York

8:1851   11 Apr 1845
LAHMANN? [LUHMANN?], Therese, wife of Valentin HOEF-
   FIGER; with 6 children
Guebwiller/ditto   Philadelphia

8:1853   12 Apr 1845
FREYBOURGER, Joseph, age 35, day laborer
Traubach-le-Bas/ditto   Canada

8:1860   17 Apr 1845
DANEOURT? [DANCOURT?], Sigismond, age 41, landowner;
   with wife & 2 children
Croix/ditto   Texas

8:1862   19 Apr 1845
MEYER, Jean, age 29, farmer; with wife & --?
Sondernach/ditto   New York

8:1863   22 Apr 1845
DIETAMANN, JeanThiebaud, age 27, weaver
Traubach-le-Bas/ditto   Canada

8:1864   24 Apr 1845
EUHER? [EICHES?], Daniel, age 20, farmer
Pulversheim?/Staffelfelden   Ohio

8:1866   24 Apr 1845
KLINGER, Jean, age 28, day laborer
--/Hausen? [Mulhausen?]   New York

4

8:1873   26 Apr 1845
ROTZELEUR, Joseph, age 20, day laborer
Faverois/ditto   New York

8:1874   26 Apr 1845
BIRRER, Nicolas, age 28, day laborer; with wife &
    2 children
Bourbach-le-Bas/ditto   New York

8:1875   25 Apr 1845
JENN, Thiebaud, age 32, day laborer; with wife &
    3 children
Bourbach-le-Bas/ditto   New York

8:1876   26 Apr 1845
GREWEY? [GREIVEY?], Nicolas, age 30, tailor
Schweighausen/ditto   New York

8:1885   02 May 1845
BOETSCH, Andre, age 50, day laborer
Vieux Ferrette/ditto   New York

8:1886   05 May 1845
ROUECHE, Richard Nicolas, age 34, farmer
Angeot/ditto   Charleston, America

8:1887   05 May 1845
MARTIN, Francois Joseph, age 43, blacksmith?
Retzviller/ditto   Charleston, America

8:1888   05 May 1845
MADRU, Jean Baptiste, age 36, farmer
--/Retzviller? or Angeot?   Charleston, America

8:1896   07 May 1845
HORNY, Gaspard, age 34, --?; with wife & 2 children
Urbes/Huseren [Husseren]   Pittsbourg [Pittsburgh]

8:1897   09 May 1845
FREYBOURGER, Francois Joseph, age 50, day laborer
Traubach-le-Bas/ditto   Canada

8:1899   07 May 1845
GULLY, Joseph, age 32, --?
--/[St.] Amarin   New York

8:1906   10 May 1845
KEMPF, Marie Agathe, age 25, businesswoman?
--/Nebirstrup?   Ohio

8:1908   10 May 1845
SUTTER, Aloyse, age 26, mechanic
Biederthal [Switzerland]/ditto   New York

8:1909   10 May 1845
GEYMANN, Aloyse, age 22, shoemaker
Biederthal [Switzerland]/ditto   New York

8:1914   13 May 1845
PAULIN, Xavier, age 39, worker --?; with wife & 7
    children
Kruth/Rouffach   New York

8:1917   15 May 1845
TURCK?, Martin, age 40, shoemaker
Kiehlingspergen [Kiechlinsbergen], Baden/Colmar
                                          New York

8:1923   16 May 1845
FREUDENREICH? Martin, age 41, cooper; with wife & 4
    children
Eguisheim/Husseren   New York

8:1924   16 May 1845
SPECHT, Michel, age 56, shoemaker; with wife & 2
    children
Urbes/Husseren   New York

8:1928   16 May 1845
BALTENWECK?, Marie Catherine, age 33, linen draper
Colmar/ditto   St. Alfonse, America

8:1930   16 May 1845
GOEPFERT, Jacques, age 35, tailor; with wife & 7
    children
Feldbach/ditto   New York

8:1932   16 May 1845
LOPINOT?, Francois, age 27, weaver
Grandvillars/ditto   New York

8:1934   17 May 1845
SCHILL, Jean Baptiste, age 38, --?; with wife, 2
    children, & maid
Waltighoffen/Ferrette   New York

8:1937   21 May 1845
KALTENBACH, Louis, age 28, designer?
Ruelisheim/ditto   Oberensville, America

8:1945   24 May 1845
STAEMPFLI, Joseph, age 42, farmer; with 5 children
Buren, Switzerland/Mulhausen   Cinzinaddi [Cin-
                                   cinnati], America

8:1946   26 May 1845
SCHMITT, Jean Pierre, age 25, carpenter
Jonchery/ditto   New York

8:1947   26 May 1845
BOETSCH, Joseph, age 29, day laborer
Vieux Ferrette/ditto   New York

8:1950   26 May 1845
WALTER, Jean, age 25, sawyer; with wife & 1 child
Vieux Ferrette/ditto   New York

5

8:1951   26 May 1845
KAYSER, Joseph, age 30, farmer
St. Ulrich/ditto   New York

8:1952   27 May 1845
SCHINDLER, Xavier, age 20, shoemaker
Traubach-le-Haut/ditto   Canada

8:1953   27 May 1845
AESTLY? [RESTLY?], Jean, age 32, wagoner
Mulhausen/ditto   Cinzinatti [Cincinatti] America

8:1957   30 May 1845
GIRARDOT, Francois, age 45, day laborer
Faverois/ditto   New Orleans

8:1958   30 May 1845
MEYER, Francois Ulric, age 35, farmer; with wife
St. Amarin/Felleringen   New York

8:1962   02 Jun 1845
GEISS, Sebastien, age 47?, postman?
Uffheim/ditto   New York

8:1963   02 Jun 1845
BOBENRIETH, Francois Antoine, age 39, shoemaker1 with
   wife & 2 children
Vileren?/ditto   New York

8:1966   03 Jun 1845
HEITZEMANN, Louis, age 18, day laborer
Magny/Montreux --?   New York

8:1967   03 Jun 1845
CHARPIAT, Francois Joseph, age 20, tailor
Faverois/ditto   New Orleans

8:1968   03 Jun 1845
ILTIS?, Jean Baptiste --?, age 28, tile maker
Hattstatt/Colmar   New York

8:1969   05 Jun 1845
SCHILDER, Martin, age 19, wheelwright; with father
   Andre Ludwig SCHILDER
Harlisheim/ditto   Schilicada, America
                                [Chillicothe?]

8:1990   11 Jun 1845
FREY, Jean, age 33, farmer; with wife & 1 child
Strasbourg/Mulhausen   New York

8:2003   17 Jun 1845
BLASIARD, Jean, age 21, laborer
Traubach-le-Bas/ditto   Canada

8:2005   20 Jun 1845
GSCHWIND, Pierre, age 32, engraver?; with wife, 3
   children, & sister-in-law
Folgenspurg/Bornach? [Rornach?]   New Orleans

8:2023   30 Jun 1845
GUILLAUME, Antoine, age 24, metal turner
Thann/ditto   New York

8:2025   30 Jun 1845
GUILLAUME, Henry, age 32, cooper
Thann/ditto   New York

8:2035   04 Jul 1845
DREYER, Jacques, age 28, day laborer
Weckolsheim?/ditto   Jefferson, America

8:2057   17 Jul 1845
LOEWENGUTH, Georges, age 30, --?; with brother
Schwalwiller?, Bas-Rhin/Thann   New York

8:2061   19 Jul 1845
HABETROH? [HABERSTROH?], Jean, age 21, spinner
Roppeviller, Moselle?/ditto   New Orleans

8:2063   21 Jul 1845
BOURGUNIOT, Julie, age 27
Giromagny/ditto   U.S.A.

8:2064   21 Jul 1845
ZIMMERMANN, Elise, age 43
Norsingen, Baden/Kayserberg   New Orleans

8:2069   24 Jul 1845
KIEMBLER?, Francois Xavier, age 22, baker
Lachapelle-sous-Chaux/Belfort   New Orleans

8:2070   24 Jul 1845
GIRARDEY, Barbe, age 54, baker
St. Amarin/ditto   Augusta, America

8:2078   26 Jul 1845
WURSTEISSEN, Marie Anne, widow of Martin, age 55;
   with 3 children
Mulhausen/ditto   New York

8:2079   26 Jul 1845
ROTH, Jean, age 26, counterminer?
Kirchberg/ditto   New York

8:2085   30 Jul 1845
FUNK, Henry, age 26, spinner
Werdenscheil, Switzerland/ditto   New York

8:2098   05 Aug 1845
BLUSS, Jean, age 47, farmer; with wife & 5? children
Niderwiller --?/Soultz   Candy? [Landy?], America

8:2099   05 Aug 1845
TSCHEILLER, Louis Charles Victor, age 35, designer
Thann/ditto   New York

8:2102   05 Aug 1845
WEISS, Charles, age 29, baker
Mulhausen/ditto   New Orleans

8:2108   08 Aug 1845
DOLLFUS, Jean Friedrich? [or Junior?], age 22, busi-
    nessman
Mulhausen/ditto   New York

8:2129   20 Aug 1845
LINZENBOLTZ? [LINZENHOLTZ?], Auguste?, age 28, spin-
    ner of cotton
Krautergersheim, Bas-Rhin/ditto   Albany, America

8:2130   20 Aug 1845
HALLER, Barbe, age 43, dressmaker
Jebsheim/Mulhausen   Philadelphia

8:2133   20 Aug 1845
MARSOT, Alexis, age 54, farmer
Chaux/ditto   New Orleans

8:2135   23 Aug 1845
CHAPPE, Xavier, age 45; with wife & 2 children
--/Denney   New York

8:2144   25 Aug 1845
MUNSCH, Pierre, age 27, day laborer
Felleringen/ditto   Mexico

8:2146   25 Aug 1845
EHLINGER, Christine, age 31, dressmaker
Storckensohn? [Horckensohn?]/Bitschwiller New Orleans

8:2153   20 Aug 1845
MARCHAND, Joseph, age 32, farmer
Boron/Bitschwiller   New York

8:2154   29 Aug 1845
RUDLER, Antoine, age 21, metal turner
Bitschwiller/ditto   New York

8:2156   01 Sep 1845
FROMALD, Pierre, age 34, cloth? printer; with wife
Thann/ditto   Philadelphia

8:2159   03 Sep 1845
KIRCHMEYER, Dominique, age 28, furniture maker?
Thann/ditto   New York

8:2161   03 Sep 1845
NEUHART, Michel, age 25, metal turner
Kutzenhausen?, Bas-Rhin/Colmar   New York

8:2162   03 Sep 1845
HAUCK, George, age 26, --?
Cernay/ditto   New York

8:2163   04 Sep 1845
SCHMIDT, Jean Martin, age 27, sawyer; with wife &
    1 child
Merwiller, Bas-Rhin?/Mulhausen   New Orleans

8:2164   04 Sep 1845
INGOLD, Dominique Napoleon, age 39, sawyer
Soultz/ditto   New York

8:2165   04 Sep 1845
FUCHS, Catherine, age 30, factory worker
Mulhausen/ditto   New Orleans

8:2166   04 Sep 1845
DIETRICH, Thiebaud, age 39, --?; with wife, child? &
    maid
Thann/ditto   Texas

8:2169   05 Sep 1845
HANTZ, Helene, age 33, worker
Rechesy/Bitschwiller   New York

8:2170   05 Sep 1845
HANTZ, Elisabeth, age 37, worker
Rechesy/Bitschwiller   New York

8:2171   05 Sep 1845
DIETERLE, Jean, age 21, tilemaker
Ingersheim/ditto   New York

8:2176   09 Sep 1845
WAPLER, Emile, age 25, businessman
Strasbourg/ditto   New Orleans

8:2177   09 Sep 1845
HUG, Francois Ignace, age 31, farmer
Aspach-le-Bas/Cernay   Caracas, [Venezuela]

8:2180   10 Sep 1845
KIEFFER, Michel, age 28, ropemaker
Kutzenhausen, Bas-Rhin/Mulhausen   New York

8:2182   10 Sep 1845
JACQUEMIN, Jean Baptiste, age 36, sawyer; with wife &
    4 children
Senones, Vosges/Guebwiller   Littelfals, America

8:2183   10 Sep 1845
FAURE, Joseph, age 38, day laborer
Auxelles-Bas/ditto   Caracas, [Venezuela]

8:2188   15 Sep 1845
WEIDENPFUL? [WADENPFUL?], Nicolas, age 20, tailor
Mulhausen/ditto   New York

8:2189   15 Sep 1845
ROTHMUND, Pierre, ae 21?, tailor of --?
Guebwiller/ditto   Littelfals, America

8:2192   16 Sep 1845
BARDOT, Charles, age 24, farmer
--/Sermamagny   New York

8:2200   19 Sep 1845
UNTERNAHR, Jean Nepomucene, age 43, farmer; with wife
   & 3 children
Buhl/ditto   Caracas, [Venezuela]

8:2207   24 Sep 1845
BUERRER, Joseph, age 28, metal turner
Thann/Bitschwiller   New York

8:2208   24 Sep 1845
SOEHNLEN, Thiebaud, age 40, weaver
Bourbach-le-Bas/ditto   New York

8:2209   24 Sep 1845
SOEHNLEN, Sebastien, age 39, day laborer; with wife &
   2 children
Bourbach-le-Bas/ditto   New York

8:2212   26 Sep 1845
PERROT, Ferdinand Francois, age 24, farmer; with wife
   & sister
Sermamagny/ditto   New York

8:2217   30 Sep 1845
BURRER, Charles, age 19, sawyer
Thann/ditto   New York

8:2229   04 Oct 1845
MULLER, Jacques, age 42, carpenter; with nephew
Neuwiller/ditto   Cincinnati

8:2230   04 Oct 1845
BOEGLIN, Jean, age 26, tailor
Ruschwiller? [Ruscheville?]/ditto [or Neuwiller]
                                       Cincinnati

8:2231   04 Oct 1845
BOIGY, Joseph, age 33, wheelwright; with wife & 4
   children
Neuwiller/ditto   Cincinnati

8:2232   04 Oct 1845
LIBSIG, Antoine, age 42, day laborer; with wife & 2
   children
Neuwiller/ditto   Cincinnati

8:2239   08 Oct 1845
ALBRECHT, Francois, age 32, cloth printer; with wife
   & 3 children
Thann/ditto   New York

8:2241   10 Oct 1845
LEINS? Josephine, wife of -- MERCKLEN, age 44, fac-
   tory worker; with daughter
Weitingen, Wuerttemberg/Thann   New York

8:2242   10 Oct 1845
WILLIEN, Marie Anne, wife of -- LIEGNIAC?, age 34,
   factory worker
Thann/ditto   New York

8:2243   10 Oct 1845
ENGELHART, Frederic, age 23, day laborer; with wife &
   2 children
Altenstatt, Bas-Rhin/ditto   New York

8:2352   14 Sep 1845
HIRTZLIN, Joseph?, age 43, farmer; with wife & 3
   children
Neuwiller/ditto   Cincinnati

8:2354   13 Oct 1845
LEMAIRE, Josephine, age 21, farmer (coloniste)
Battenheim/Mulhausen   New York

8:2361   18 Oct 1845
HANSBERGER, Joseph, age 37, blacksmith
Bitschwiller/ditto   New York

8:2362   18 Oct 1845
MISSLAND, Jean, age 24, metal turner
Bitschwiller/ditto   New York

8:2365   21 Oct 1845
KOLB, Gaspard, Junior?, age 20, manufacturer
Rammersmatt/ditto   New York

8:2366   21 Oct 1845
KOOS, Joseph, age 31, manufacturer
Rammersmatt/ditto   New York

8:2367   22 Oct 1845
SPECK, Nicolas, age 40, spinner
Bitschwiller/ditto   New York

8:2368   22 Oct 1845
EHRET, Francois Joseph, age 20, spinner?
Oberbruck/Rammersmatt   New York

8:2369   22 Oct 1845
BOSSLER, Antoine, age 62, day laborer; with wife & 2
   children
Bourbach-le-Bas/ditto   New York

8:2375   27 Oct 1845
STUCKER, Thiebaud, age 58, miner?; with wife & 3
   children
Rammersmatt/ditto   New York

8:2379   29 Oct 1845
WICKY, Joseph, age 36, weaver; with wife & 3 children
Kirchberg/Bourbach-le-Bas   New York

8:2386   31 Oct 1845
EHRET, Antoine, age 45, --; with wife, 6 children, &
   granddaughter
Rammersmatt/ditto   New York

8:2387   31 Oct 1845
WEBER, Sylvestre, age 23, bookbinder?
Husseren/ditto   New Orleans

8:2390   05 Nov 1845
GISSINGES? [GISSINGER?], Joseph, age 33, mason
Carspach/Chapelle-s?-Rougemont   New York

8:2396   06 Nov 1845
REICH, Pierre Antoine, age 61, farmer; with daughter
   Eve, age 20
Salmbach, Bas-Rhin/Mulhouse   New Orleans

8:2397   08 Nov 1845
FAHRNER? [FUHRNER?], Jean Michel, age 35, weaver;
   with wife & 2 children
Baldenheim, Bas-Rhin/ Ste. Croix aux M[ines]
                              St. Louis, America

8:2398   08 Nov 1845
FAHRNER? [FUHRNER?], Andre, age 28, weaver; with wife
   & 2 children
Baldenheim, Bas-Rhin/Ste. Croix aux M[ines]
                              St. Louis, America

8:2399   08 Nov 1845
FAHRNER? [FUHRNER?], Francois Joseph, age 40, weaver
Baldenheim, Bas-Rhin/Ste. Croix aux M[ines]
                              St. Louis, America

8:2400   08 Nov 1845
GURMELY, Francois, age 45, weaver; with wife & 2
   children
Liepvre/Ste. Croix aux M[ines]   St. Louis, America

8:2401   08 Nov 1845
SCHIFFMACHER, Leonard, age 52, farmer; with daughter?
   & grandchildren?
Scheidenhard?/Mulhausen   New Orleans

8:2403   10 Nov 1845
MATTHIEU, Marie Anne, age 21, seamstress
Ste. Croix aux Mines/ditto   St. Louis, America

8:2406   13 Nov 1845
CACHOT, Dominique, age 46, --; with wife & 2 children
Granges, Vosges/Bitschwiller   New York

8:2410   13 Nov 1845
ROOS, Joseph, age 23, edge-tool maker
Willer/ditto   Philadelphia

8:2411   17 Nov 1845
MEYER, Sebastien, age 43, weaver; with wife & 7 chil-
   dren
Bourbach-le-Bas/ditto   New York

8:2419   22 Nov 1845
URBAIN, Jean Nicolas, age 27, farmer
Ste. Croix aux Mines/ditto   St. Louis, America

8:2420   24 Nov 1845
GASPERMENT, Joseph, age 19, farmer
Ste. Croix aux Mines/ditto   St. Louis, America

8:2428   27 Nov 1845
WUEHLINGER? [STUEHLINGER?], Jacques, age 55, tinsmith
Alzey, Hessen-Darmstadt/Colmar   New York

8:2432   29 Nov 1845
KRUST? Joseph Andre, age 28, liquor distiller
Cernay/ditto   New Orleans

8:2447   15 Nov 1845
HEISLEN, Paul, age 27, joiner; with wife & 1 child
Rouffach/ditto   Jefferson, America

8:2448   15 Nov 1845
SOHN, Ignace, ae 58, vinegrower; with wife & niece
Rouffach/ditto   Jefferson, America

8:2449   15 Nov 1845
FINCK, Antoine, age 51, mason; with wife
Langenegg, Austria/ditto   Jefferson, America

8:2452   17 Nov 1845
BIGINO, Elisabeth, age 25, cook; with 1 child
Cernay/ditto   Jefferson, America

8:2457   23 Nov 1845
BRAND, Boniface, age 30, landowner
--/Burnhaupt-le-Haut   New York

8:2458   23 Nov 1845
SPENLINHAUER, Andre, age 30, day laborer
Vieux Ferrette/ditto   New York

8:2459   23 Nov 1845
KEMPFF, Jean Baptiste, age 17, day laborer; with sis-
   ter
Niederentzen/ditto   Jefferson, America

8:2463   27 Nov 1845
BOTZY? [BOLZY?], Jean, age 37, --?
Vieux Ferrette/feldbach   New York

8:2481   07 Jan 1846
DREY, Georges, age 19, blacksmith
Durrenentzen/ditto   Chicago

8:2485   12 Jan 1846
SCHLATTER, Joseph, age 36? 30?, farmer
Heideviller/Issenheim   New York

8:2492   26 Jan 1846
HETTERLIN, Joseph, age 38, farmer
Heimersdorf/Koesttach   New York

8:2493   27 Jan 1846
RUNSER, Philippe, age 36, weaver; with wife & 6 chil-
    dren
Folgenspurg/Hegenheim   New York

8:2507   07 Feb 1846
MULLER, Georges, age 30, shoemaker; with wife, mother
    & 3 children
Koenigsschaffhausen, Baden/Jebsheim   New York

8:2512   10 Feb 1846
WITTMANN, Nicolas, age 36, shoemaker; with wife & 3
    children
Thann/ ditto   New York

8:2513   12 Feb 1846
BERG? [BIRY?], Andre, age 26, blacksmith
Bernardswiller, Obernai, Bas-Rhin/Mulhausen
                              New Orleans

8:2514   12 Feb 1846
WENDLING, Joseph, age 30, blacksmith
Willgottheim, Bas-Rhin/Mulhausen   New Orleans

8:2515   12 Feb 1846
HENNY, Francois Xavier, age 29, domestic
Bernardswiller, Obernai, Bas-Rhin/Mulhausen
                              New Orleans

8:2521   16 Feb 1846
SIFFERLEN, Thiebaud, age 46, farmer; with wife & 5
    children
Guewenheim/ditto   New York

8:2522   16 Feb 1846
PRENAT? [TRENAT?], Florentin, age 18, day laborer
Villars-le-Haut?/ditto   New York

8:2523   16 Feb 1846
PRENAT? [TRENAT?], Antoine, age 18, day laborer
Villars-le-Haut?/ditto   New York

8:2524   16 Feb 1846
HATIE, Chretien, age 22, shoemaker; with wife & child
Sentheim/Guewenheim   New York

8:2525   16 Feb 1846
BURRER? [BARRER?], Ignace, age 26, businessman; with
    wife
Guewenheim/ditto   New York

8:2526   16 Feb 1846
SCHMIT, Francois Antoine, age 29, day laborer; with
    wife & 4 children
Guewenheim/ditto   New York

8:2527   16 Feb 1846
DEGENHARD? Balthasare?, age 56, wheelwright; with
    wife & 4 children
Burnhaupt-le-Bas/ditto   New York

8:2528   16 Feb 1846
DEGENHARD, Joseph, age 33, wheelwright; with wife
Massevaux/ditto   New York

8:2529   17 Feb 1846
RICHERT, George, age 25, carpenter
Durrenentzen/ditto   New York

8:2530   17 Feb 1846
RUMMELHART, Joseph, age 24, weaver
Sternenberg [Switzerland]/ditto   Canada

8:2533   17 Feb 1846
CHATILLON, Marie Josephine, age 37, merchant?
--/Salbert? [Lalbert?]   New York

8:2535   19 Feb 1846
MADRU, Francois, age 51, farmer; with wife & 5 chil-
    dren
Angeot/ditto   Charleston, America

8:2536   19 Feb 1846
PREBHAN? [REBHAN?], Mathias, age 46, mason; with wife
    & 6 children
--/Guewenheim   New York

8:2538   19 Feb 1846
ROUECHE, Jacques Richard, age 43, landowner; with
    wife & 2 children
Angeot/ditto   Charleston, America

8:2541   20 Feb 1846
NITTERKOLLER, Joseph, age 52, courier?; with wife & 7
    children
Guewenatten/ditto   Canada

8:2546   21 Feb 1846
UMBDENSTOCK, Mathias, age 50, farmer; with wife & 3
    children
Ostheim/ditto   New York

8:2547   23 Feb 1846
SCHALLENBERGER, Jacques, age 40, joiner?
Voegthinshoffen/Ste.-Croix-aux-Mines New York

8:2549   23 Feb 1846
VETTER, Joachim, age 32, shoemaker
Sondersdorff/ditto   Cincinnati

8:2550   23 Feb 1846
BLONDE, Joseph, age 17? 18?, farmer
Guewenatten/ditto   Canada

8:2554   27 Feb 1846
DROZ, Francois, age 31, farmer; with wife & 1 child
Chaux/ditto   New Orleans

8:2555   27 Feb 1846
LAVAL, Jerome, age 40, farmer; with wife & 3 children
Chaux/ditto   New Orleans

8:2556   27 Feb 1846
FREYBARGER? [FREYBURGER?], Jean, age 45, farmer; with
    wife & 3? children
Traubach-le-Bas/ditto   Canada

8:2558   27 Feb 1846
LORENTZ, Jean, age 51, day laborer; with wife & 5?
    children
Sternenberg [Switzerland]/ditto   New York

8:2559   27 Feb 1846
THOMANN, Clement, age 29, day laborer
Ostheim/ditto   New York

8:2561   27 Feb 1846
BERGDOLL, Joseph, age 46, driver
Roppeviller, Moselle/ditto   New Orleans

8:2563   28 Feb 1846
LAMBOLE, Francois Joseph, age 20, farmer; with bro-
    ther
Angeot/ditto   Charleston, America

8:2566   03 Mar 1846
BANDSTETTER, Jacques, age 25, wheelwright
Ferrette/ditto   New Orleans

8:2567   03 Mar 1846
LITZLER, Meinrad, age 24, saddler?
Oberdorff/ditto   New York

8:2569   03 Mar 1846
CHANEY, Marie, wife of Joseph MARCHAND, age 29, fac-
    tory worker; with daughter
Bretagne/Bitschwiller   New York

8:2570   03 Mar 1846
SCHOFFMANN, Joseph, age 38, farmer; with wife & 7
    children
Traubach-le-Haut/ditto   New York

8:2571   03 Mar 1846
DORMOIS, Pierre Christophe, age 23, spinner
Hericourt, Haute-Saone/thann   New York

8:2577   04 Mar 1846
CHATELOT, Francois, age 28, joiner
--/Essert   New York

8:2579   04 Mar 1846
WETZEL, Francois Joseph, age 29, servant
Angeot/Burnhaupt-le-Bas   New York

8:2584   05 Mar 1846
GROSHAENY, Christian, age 23, cook
Habsheim/Thann   New York

8:2585   05 Mar 1846
MARCHAND, Justin Desire, age 24, farmer
Chapelle-sous-Chaux/Sermamagny   New Orleans

8:2591   07 Mar 1846
ROY, Nicolas, age 22, armer
Angeot/ditto   Charleston, America

8:2593   07 Mar 1846
WIRTH, Nicolas, age 31, --?; with wife & 5 children
Galsingen/Bermviller   New York

8:2595   07 Mar 1846
WADEL, Joseph, age 40, manufacturer; with wife, 4
    children, & mother
Ammerzwiller/Riefmatten   Ohio

8:2598   09 Mar 1846
PFLEGER, Jean, age 31, --; with wife & 2 children
Friessen/ditto   New York

8:2603   13 Mar 1846
GROSJEAN, Michel, age 22, blacksmith
Bitschwiller/ditto   New York

8:2604   14 Mar 1846
BESANCON, Francois, age 49, farmer; with wife & 3
    children
Denney/ditto   New York

8:2605   14 Mar 1846
FREYENBERGER, Isaac, age 28, farmer
Blotzheim/ditto   New York

8:2608   16 Mar 1846
SETTELEN, Francois Antoine, age 26, tailor
Wittenheim/ditto   Mexico

8:2615   18 Mar 1846
ROTH, Barbe, age 28, servant
Brumstatt? [Brunnstatt?]/Blotzheim   New York

8:2618   18 Mar 1846
KLEPFFENSTEIN? [KLOPFENSTEIN?], Jean, age 19, farmer
Leymen/Ostheim   New York

8:2624   19 Mar 1846
DESDAMES? RESDAMES?, Nicolas, age 27, farmer
Roppe/ditto   New York

8:2625   19 Mar 1846
CUYOT? [CAYOT?], Georges, age 38, farmer; with wife &
    4 children
Pfaffau/Roppe   New York

8:2628   19 Mar 1846
GUILLINGER, Marguerite, age 21, maid; with 1 child
Soppe-le-Haut/ditto   New York

8:2629   21 Mar 1846
BONAT, Nicolas, age 28, farmer
Roppe/ditto   New York

8:2631   24 Mar 1846
PONCE, Francois, age 20, farmer
Roppe/ditto   New York

8:2632   25 Mar 1846
FOURNIER, Francois Joseph, age 19, farmer
Ammertzviller/Guewenheim   New York

8:2633   25 Mar 1846
CUYOT? [CAYOT?], Pierre, age 18, farmer
Roppe/ditto   New York

8:2635   25 Mar 1846
WIEKERSHEIM? [WICKERSHEIM?], Michel, age 41, weaver;
    with wife & 5 children
Ostheim/ditto   New York

8:2636   25 Mar 1846
STAHL, Marg]aret]te, wife of -- WAPLER, age 52, wea-
    ver; with grandchildren & --?
Strasbourg/Mulhausen   New Orleans

8:2640   28 Mar 1846
FLEURY, Joseph, age 19, merchant
Le Truix?/ditto   Philadelphia

8:2641   28 Mar 1846
DUCLOUX, Pierre Nicolas, age 20, day laborer
Faverois/ditto   New Orleans

8:2642   28 Mar 1846
MAITRE, Francois Laurent, age 19, weaver
Faverois/ditto   New Orleans

8:2643   30 Mar 1846
FISCHER, George, age 29, farmer
Kuenheim/ditto   New York

8:2644   30 Mar 1846
BARTENBACH, David, age 22, farmer
Kuenheim/ditto   New York

8:2645   30 Mar 1846
HUNSINGER, Jean Jacques, age 29, farmer
Kuenheim/Wolffgantzen   New York

8:2646   31 Mar 1846
FAIVRE, Louis, age 49, farmer
Rechotte/ditto   New York

8:2647   31 Mar 1846
BERTIN? [BERLIN?], Jacques, age 20? 24?, farmer
Faverois/ditto   New York

8:2648   31 Mar 1846
FAIVRE, Francois, age 23, farmer
Rechotte/ditto   New York

8:2664   04 Apr 1846
LATSCH, Etienne Sebastien, age 36, farmer
Lewin? [Sewen?]/Massevaux   New York

8:2669   06 Apr 1846
CHARTON, Pierre, age 37, spinner; with wife & 3 chil-
    dren
Blamont, Doubs/Bitschwiller   New York

8:2674   07 Apr 1846
KNAUSS, Jean Frederic, age 59, vine grower; with wife
    & 4 children
Mittelwihr/ditto   New York

8:2675   07 Apr 1846
SCHALLER, Jean Jacques, age 54, vine grower; with
    wife & 1 child
Mittelwihr/ditto   New York

8:2676   07 Apr 1846
DUPRE, Jean Pierre, age 28, wheelwright; with wife &
    2 children
--/Roppe   New York

8:2678   08 Apr 1846
GRAWEY, Jean, age 33, cotton spinner; with wife & 2
    children
Hecken/Thann   New York

8:2680   11 Apr 1846
BURLEN, Sebastien, age 36 vine grower
Bennwihr/ditto   Chicago

8:2681   11 Apr 1846
KNITTEL, Pierre Louis, age 54, vine grower; with wife
    & 5 children
Bennwihr/ditto   Chicago

8:2685   15 Apr 1846
KNAUSS? [KRAUSS?], Geoffroi, age 54, ropemaker; with
    wife & 2 children & servant
Colmar/ditto   New York

8:2688   16 Apr 1846
BLISS, Jean Baptiste, age not given, servant
Grussenheim? [Grassenheim?]/ditto   New York

8:2694   18 Apr 1846
MONSHEIM, Augustin, age 42, farmer; with wife
Ostheim/ditto   New York

8:2699   20 Apr 1846
AUDRAN, Guillaume, age 63, former notary
Dannemarie/Mulhausen   New York

8:2700   20 Apr 1846
SCHOEN, Francois Pierre, age 44, former notary; with
    wife & 4 children
Traubach-le-Haut/ditto   New York

8:2701   20 Apr 1846
MELLECKER, Joseph, age 22, joiner
Guevenatten/Soppe-le-Bas   New York

8:2706   23 Apr 1846
DIESTELRATH, Guillaume, age 43, tailor
Niderluzingen?, Prussia/Mulhausen   New York

8:2708   23 Apr 1846
HAGER, George, age 29, weaver; with wife & 2 children
Schweighausen? [Schwaighausen?/ditto   Ohio

8:2709   23 Apr 1846
HABERTHUR, Nicolas, age 28, weaver; with wife & 2
    children
Schweighausen? [Schwaighausen?]/ditto   Ohio

8:2711   24 Apr 1846
JACQUEMIN, Pierre Laiz?, age 21, musician
Foussemagne/Vezelois   New York

8:2712   24 Apr 1846
JACQUEMIN, Francois Xavier, age 24, shoemaker
Vezelois/ditto   New York

8:2713   24 Apr 1846
WALLER, Joseph, age 42, shoemaker
Seppois-le-Bas/ditto   New York

8:2714   24 Apr 1846
SCHIRCK, Anne Marie, age 30, shoemaker?
Seppois-le-Bas/ditto   New York

8:2719   27 Apr 1846
WALLIS, Jules, age 15, --
Paris/Colmar   New York

8:2732   30 Apr 1846
ROYER, Francois Joseph, age 35, landowner
Bavilliers/ditto   New York

8:2733   30 Apr 1846
HAGER, Jean Thiebaud, age 65, cooper; with wife & 5
    children
Schweighausen/ditto   Ohio

8:2734   30 Apr 1846
ERHARD, Joseph, age 27, farmer
Ueberstrass/ditto   New York

8:2737   02 May 1846
BECK, Michel, age 38, former military
Carspach/ditto   New York

8:2738   02 May 1846
HORNUNG, Jean, age 30, farmer
Wolschwiller/ditto   New York

8:2740   02 May 1846
JUEN, Joseph, age 23, farmer
Wolfschwiller/ditto   New York

8:2741   02 May 1846
TONDRE, George, age 19, furniture maker?
--/Eteimbes? [Etobon?]   New York

8:2742   04 May 1846
PIQUEREZ, Marie Annie, age 24, dressmaker
Meroux/ditto   New York

8:2745   04 May 1846
EHLINGER, Salome? [Salomon?], age 22, factory worker
Willer/ditto   New York

8:2746   04 May 1846
EHLINGER, Marie Anne, wife of -- MISSLAND?, age 24,
    factory worker
Willer/ditto   New York

8:2748   05 May 1846
REITTER? [RUTTER?], Jacques, age 24, vine grower
Hunerwihr?/ditto   New York

8:2754   07 May 1846
TONDRE?[TENDRE?], Conrad, age 20, cooper
--/Eteimbes? [Etobon?]   New York

8:2756   08 May 1846
ABRY, Jean George, age 33, carpenter
Riguewihr/Ste.-Marie-aux-Mines   New Orleans

8:2758   08 May 1846
LESTER, Ignace, age 46, master weaver; with wife & 3
    children
Schweighausen/ditto   Ohio

8:2768   11 May 1846
STANISIERE, Jean Baptiste, ae 20, worker
Liepvre/ditto   New Orleans

8:2769   11 May 1846
LITIQUE, Nicolas, age 27, tailor
Ste.-Croix-aux-Mines/ditto   St. Louis, America

8:2770   11 May 1846
MEYER, Georges, age 23, day laborer
Traubach-le-Bas/ditto   Canada

8:2771   11 May 1846
FRECHARD? Jean Baptiste, age 25, joiner
Liepvre/ditto   New Orleans

8:2774   12 May 1846
DROZ, George, age 22, farmer
Chaux/ditto   New Orleans

8:2775   12 May 1846
DUVIE, Conrad, age 20, worker
Liepvre/ditto   New Orleans

8:2776   12 May 1846
JACQUOT, Marie Catherine, wife of -- JACQUOT, age 23,
    --; with 1 daughter
Liepvre/ditto   New Orleans

8:2777   12 May 1846
VALDEJO, Sebastien, age 19, wheelwright; with? Jac-
    ques WEISS, age 30
Liepvre/ditto   New Orleans

8:2791   18 May 1846
DANHEISER? [DANHEISES?], Michel, age 27, merchant
Saverne, Bas-Rhin/Bergheim   New Orleans

8:2803   23 May 1846
BUSSLER, Joseph, age 45, framer; with wife & 3 chil-
    dren
Traubach-le-Haut/ditto   New York

8:2805   23 May 1846
WEY, Jean, age 23, day laborer
Bourbach-le-Bas/Burnhaupt-le-Haut   New York

8:2807   23 May 1846
STAFFELBACH, Ignace, age 47, farmer; with wife & 4?
    children
Burnhaupt-le-Haut/ditto   New York

8:2808   23 May 1846
GERTHOFER*, Ignace, age 32, farmer; with wife & 2
    children
Burnhaupt-le-Haut/ditto   New York
*So spelled.

8:2809   23 May 1846
GERTHOFFER?* [GERHOFFES?], Francois Joseph, age 34,
    farmer
Burnhaupt-le-Haut/ditto   New York
*So spelled.

8:2810   25 May 1846
WIESER, Joseph, age 4o, driver
Niederbruck/Lame?   New York

8:2824   27 May 1846
FOLLOT, Joseph, age 41, watchmaker
Sermamagny/ditto   New York

8:2831   29 May 1846
ERHARD, Joseph, age 26, blacksmith
Willer, Canton de Thann/ditto   New York

8:2837   02 Jun 1846
DIETEMANN, Joseph age 36, farmer
Traubach-le-Haut/ditto   New York

8:2842   03 Jun 1846
DAEGELEN, Xavier, age 40, mayor?; with wife, 5 chil-
    dren, father, and sister
--/Guewenheim   New York

8:2843   03 Jun 1846
WENDLING, Andre, age 40, blacksmith; with wife, 9
    children, and brother
--/Guewenheim   New York

8:2846   04 Jun 1846
BIHL, Anee Marie, age 22, --?
Brechaumont/ditto   New York

8:2853   05 Jun 1846
HUG, Joseph, age 33, day laborer; with wife & 5?
    children
Traubach-le-Haut/ditto   Caracas, Venezuela

8:2854   06 Jun 1846
SCHILLIG, Paul, age 53, da laborer; with wife & 7?
    children
Traubach-le-Haut/ditto   Caracas, Venezuela

8:2855   06 Jun 1846
HECKLY, Joseph, age 36, day laborer; with wife & 3
    children
Guevenatten/ditto   Caracas, Venezuela

8:2856   06 Jun 1846
WALTER, Marie Madeleine, age --?, day laborer; with 2
    children
Traubach-le-Haut/ditto   Caracas, Venezuela

8:2857   06 Jun 1846
NIEDERKOHLER, Jean, age 41, messenger?; with wife & 4
    children
Guevenatten/ditto   Caracas, Venezuela

8:2858   08 Jun 1846
GROS, Pierre Francois, age 50, landowner; with wife &
    8 children
Vaulte?-des-Mont/ditto   New York

8:2859   08 Jun 1846
JELIDON, Francois, age 40, landowner; with wife & 6
    children
Vaulte?-des-Mont/ditto   New York

8:2860   08 Jun 1846
BITSCH, Joseph, age 46, day laborer; with wife & 3
    children
Traubach-le-Haut/ditto   New York

14

8:2865   09 Jun 1846
NEUBAUER, Catherine, age 23, --
Lembach, Bas-Rhin/Niderbergheim   New York

8:2871   12 Jun 1846
KUHN, Francois, age 52, --?
Ruestenhart/ditto   St. Alphonse, Norwalk, America

8:2873   12 Jun 1846
MEINSOHN, Francois Joseph, age 35, farmer
--/Cernay   New Orleans

8:2874   12 Jun 1846
HAAS, Ignace, age 23, day laborer
Burnhaupt-le-Haut/ditto   New York

8:2886   15 Jun 1846
ZENGERLE, Reantaire?, age 44, mason; with wife & 1
   child
Schnapfen?, Austria/Thann   New York

8:2889   16 Jun 1846
BURRER, Catherine, age 22, --?
Thann/ditto   New York

8:2890   17 Jun 1846
MEINSOHN, Jean Baptiste, age 24, farmer
--/Cernay   New Orleans

8:2894   18 Jun 1846
KUENEMANN, Thiebaud, age 43, weaver; with wife, 8
   children, and sister-in-law
Rammersmatt/ditto   New York

8:2895   20 Jun 1846
SCHNAITER?, Jean Ernest, age 38, health officer
Broggingen, Baden/Colmar   New York

8:2900   23 Jun 1846
ALTHOFER?, Damien, age 38, vine grower; with wife & 1
   child
Artzenheim/Hegenheim   Philadelphia

8:2901   24 Jun 1846
STUCKY, Nicolas, age 55, farmer; with wife & 5? chil-
   dren
Staffelfelden/Rorschach?-le-Bas   New York

8:2902   24 Jun 1846
STUCKY, Barbe, widow of -- SCHLATTER?, age 4-?, far-
   mer; with 2 children
Pfafstatt?/Rorschach?-le-Bas   New York

8:2905   25 Jun 1846
STOUFF, Jean Pierre, age 60, day laborer; with wife &
   4? children
Florimont/ditto   New York

8:2911   27 Jun 1846
SCHAEFOTT? [SCHAEFOLT?], Jean Baptiste, age 39, land-
owner
Ribeauville/ditto   New York

8:2912   27 Jun 1846
BATOT, Jean, age 40, day laborer; with wife & 4 chil-
   dren
--/Mittelwihr   Texas

8:2913   27 Jun 1846
HANTZ, Jean Jacques, age 42, day laborer; with wife &
   5 children
--/Mittelwihr   Texas

8:2914   27 Jun 1846
WECKER, Jean George, age 35, day laborer; with wife &
   1 child
--/Mittelwihr   Texas

8:2919   29 Jun 1846
REBISCHON, Thiebaud, age 49, engraver
Villefranche, [Rhein?]/Mulhausen   Providence

8:2922   02 Jul 1846
STUCKER, Ambroise, age 50, miner; with wife & 7 chil-
   dren
Rammersmatt/ditto   New York

8:2923   02 Jul 1846
STUCKER, Francois, age 41, miner; with wife & 3 chil-
   dren
Rammersmatt/ditto   New York

8:2928   02 Jul 1846
MEYER, Henriette, age 22, --?
Mulhausen/ditto   Texas

8:2931   03 Jul 1846
WENDLING, Jean Thiebaut, age 33, blacksmith; with
   wife
Michelbach?/ditto   New York

8:2934   04 Jul 1846
LENHERR?, Jeanne, age 21, dressmaker
St. Louis/ditto   Texas

8:2937   06 Jul 1846
SCHMITT, Christine, age 24, --?; with 1 child
Felleringen/ditto   Philadelphia

8:2939   07 Jul 1846
BITSCH, Jacques, age 47, farmer
Burnhaupt-le-Bas/ditto   Venezuela

8:2941   09 Jul 1846
JODER, Simon, age 55, shoemaker?; with wife
Danjoutin/Niedermorschwiller?   New York

8:2945   10 Jul 1846
KOOS, Marie Anne, widow of -- BURRER, age 59, inn-
    keeper
Rammersmatt/Thann   New York

8:2956   16 Jul 1845
KURZMANN, Martin, age 40, factory worker; with wife,
    7 children, & sister-in-law
Ranspach/ditto   Augusta, America

8:2957   16 Jul 1846
BOBENRIETH, Anne Marie, age 46, factory worker
Ranspach/ditto   New York

8:2963   23 Jul 1846
LEVEQUE, Eduard, age 37, merchant
St. Louis/ditto   U.S.A.

8:2984   03 Aug 1846
PAYOT, Jean Claude, age 49, farmer; with wife & 6
    children
--/Roppe   St. Augustin Cecile, America

8:2985   03 Aug 1846
ZELLER, theophile, age 33, tailor; with wife & 2
    children
Plancher-Bas, Haut-Saone/Belfort   New York

8:2987   03 Aug 1846
DESDAMES, Sebastien, age 29, farmer
--/Roppe   St. Augustin Cecile, America

8:2996   07 Aug 1846
HALDY? [NALDY?], Joseph, age 40, carter; with wife &
    1 child
Eschholtzmatt, Switzerland/Oderen   New Orleans

8:2998   08 Aug 1846
GIRARDHEY, Joseph, age 47, farmer; with wife & child
Rougemont/ditto   Philadelphia

8:3000   10 Aug 1846
BAUMGARTNER, Aloise, age 50, gardener; with wife
Naggenschwill, Switzerland/Mulhausen New Orleans

8:3001   10 Aug 1846
STROBEL, George, age 40, cotton printer?; with wife
Mulhausen/ditto   New Orleans

8:3005   12 Aug 1846
KLEIN, Jacques, age 68, --?
Struth, Bas-Rhin/Thann   New Orleans

8:3006   12 Aug 1846
BLEYER, Jean David, age 29, butcher
Mittelwihr/ditto   New York

8:3007   12 Aug 1846
BLEYER, Frederic, age 26, joiner
Mittelwihr/ditto   New York

8:3012   14 Aug 1846
KOLL, Jacques, age 37, gardener
Wattwiller/ditto   Lexington, America

8:3013   14 Aug 1846
DEIBER? [DEIBES?], Jean Baptiste, age 27, gardener
Delle/ditto   Lexington, America

8:3025   21 Aug 1846
HEIBERGER, Jean, age 41, day laborer; with wife & 6
    children
Traubach-le-Bas/ditto   New York

8:3035   26 Aug 1846
PERROT, Francois Joseph, age 45, --?
Rougegoutte/ditto   New York

8:3039   27 Aug 1846
MAURER, Joseph, age 29, former rural guard
St.-Ulrich/ditto   New York

8:3040   27 Aug 1846
ESCHEMANN, Francois, age 29, farmer; with wife & 3
    children
Eguenique? [Eguenigue?]/ditto   New York

8:3041   27 Aug 1846
GRUNINGER, Laurent, age 34, landowner
Colmar/Ingenheim   New York

8:3049   29 Aug 1846
CHERAY, Francois, age 49, --?; with wife & 3 children
Bavilliers/Belfort   New Orleans

8:3054   29 Aug 1846
GERARD, Joseph, age 42, farmer
--/Liepvre   New Orleans

8:3059   02 Sep 1846
NUN, Joseph, age 40, joiner; with wife & 3 children
Thann/ditto   New York

8:3060   02 Sep 1846
LOUIS, Jacques, age 39, farmer; with wife & 5 chil-
    dren
--/Denney   New York

8:3061   02 Sep 1846
SCHNABEL, Francois, age 44, employee --?; with wife &
    2 children
Bouxwiller, Bas-Rhin/Mulhouse   Pennsylvania

8:3064   03 Aug 1846
BOURGUARD, Pierre Joseph, age 22, baker
Roppe/ditto   New York

8:3066   04 Aug 1846
HUTZLER, Antoine, age 41, farmer; with wife & 6 chil-
dren
Oberentzen/Niederentzen   Castroville? Texas

8:3071   04 Aug 1846
RIBER, Jean, age 28, farmer
Meyenheim/ditto   Texas

8:3072   04 Aug 1846
RIBER, Francois Joseph, age 26, wheelwright
Meyenheim/ditto   Texas

8:3073   04 Aug 1846
KEMPF, Antoine, age 71, carpenter
Meyenheim/ditto   Texas

8:3074   07 Sep 1846
SCHREIBER, Jean, age 44, day laborer; with wife & 3
children
Niederentzen/Oberentzen   Texas

8:3075   07 Sep 1846
FRICKER, Joseph, age 45, day laborer; with wife & 1
child
Niederentzen/ditto   Texas

8:3076   07 Sep 1846
HUTZLER, Augustin, age 38, day laborer; with wife,
sister, & 3 children
Oberentzen/ditto   Texas

8:3077   07 Sep 1846
WIPFF, Francois Joseph, age 26, joiner
Niederentzen/ditto   Texas

8:3078   07 Sep 1846
ZINSMEISTER, Hubert, age 31, joiner
Biltzheim/ditto   Texas

8:3079   07 Sep 1846
BRUCK, Sebastien, age 29, day laborer
Niederentzen/ditto   Texas

8:3080   07 Sep 1846
WIPF, Sebastien, age 18, shoemaker
Niederentzen/ditto   Texas

8:3081   07 Sep 1846
KELLER, Francois, age 28, day laborer
Oberentzen/Niederentzen   Texas

8:3082   07 Sep 1846
GARTEISEN, Jean Baptiste, age 46, carter; with bro-
ther, sister, &_4 children
Niederentzen/ditto   Texas

8:3083   07 Sep 1846
KIENER, Joseph, age 44, farmer; with wife & 5 chil-
dren
Niederentzen/ditto   Texas

8:3084   07 Sep 1846
BENDELE, Jacques, age 45, farmer; with wife & 3 chil-
dren
Ste.-Croix-en-Plaine/Niederentzen   Texas

8:3085   08 Sep 1846
FINGER, Joseph, age 30, laborer; with wife & 1 child
Oberentzen/ditto   Texas

8:3086   08 Sep 1846
KRAUSHAAR, Elisabeth, wife of -- NEUHART, age 25, --;
with 1 child
Gaebwiller/Thann   Rochester, America

8:3087   08 Sep 1846
DOPPLER, Jean, age 47, shoemaker; with wife & 2 chil-
dren
Niederhagenthal/ditto   New York

8:3089   08 Sep 1846
GAECHTER?, Georges, age 49, day laborer; with wife &
r children
Dannemarie/Traubach-le-Bas   New York

8:3090   08 Sep 1846
KELLER, Francois-Joseph, age 39, farmer; with wife &
3 children
Niederhergheim/ditto   Texas

8:3093   10 Sep 1846
NICOT, Martin, age 28, tailor
Turckheim/Mulhouse   New York

8:3094   10 Sep 1846
BECK, Francois Joseph, age 45, farmer; with nephew
--/Sentheim   New Orleans

8:3096   11 Sep 1846
HEYLANDT, Gustave Adolphe, age 34, businessman
--/Hunawihr? [Trunawihr?]   New York

8:3099   12 Sep 1846
PRENAT, Auguste, age 18, tailor
Villars-le-See? [Bas?]/ditto   New York

8:3100   12 Sep 1846
PRENAT, Joseph Peterlin?, age 16, day laborer
Villars-le-See? [Bas?]/ditto   New York

8:3101   12 Sep 1846
PRENAT, Xavier, age 18, day laborer
Villars-le-See? [Bas?]/ditto   New York

8:3102   12 Sep 1846
KIENE, Auguste, age 28, dyer
--/Rouffach   New York

8:3104   12 Sep 1846
FUERSTENBERGER, Antoine, age 50, farmer; with wife &
   6 children
--/Niederhergheim   Texas

8:3106   14 Sep 1846
SPETTEL, Jean Baptiste, age 22, blacksmith
Heiteren/ditto   Texas

8:3107   14 Sep 1846
KAUFFMANN, Jacques, age 29, farmer
Heiteren/ditto   Texas

8:3108   14 Sep 1846
BRIDEN, Andre, age 39, farmer; with wife & children
Oberentzen/ditto   Texas

8:3110   14 Sep 1846
TRANELTER? [CRANELTER?], Joseph, age 18, day laborer
Oberentzen/ditto   Texas

8:3111   14 Sep 1846
HABY, Francois Joseph, age 53, farmer; with 6 chil-
   dren
Oberentzen/ditto   Texas

8:3112   14 Sep 1846
MANN, Jean-Louis, age 19, shepherd
Oberentzen/ditto   Texas

8:3113   14 Sep 1846
SCHMITT, Xavier, age 35, joiner; with wife & 3 chil-
   dren
Oberentzen/ditto   Texas

8:3114   14 Sep 1846
RITTIMANN, Jean, age 46, laborer; with wife & 7 chil-
   dren
Oberentzen/ditto   Texas

8:3115   14 Sep 1846
GRENAT? [GRENAH?], Jean-Jacques, age 44, weaver; with
   wife, 3 children, & father-in-law
Oberentzen/ditto   New York

8:3116   14 Sep 1846
SCHMITT, Jean Michel, age 21, day laborer
Oberentzen/ditto   Texas

8:3117   14 Sep 1846
ZUERCHER, Leopold, age 25, laborer
Oberentzen/ditto   Texas

8:3118   14 Sep 1846
BIRY, Jacques, age 30, shoemaker
Oberentzen/ditto   Texas

8:3119   14 Sep 1846
AHR? [OHR?], Etienne, age 25, blacksmith
Oberentzen/ditto   Texas

8:3120   14 Sep 1846
STUDER, Georges, age 42, hunter; with wife & 2 chil-
   dren
Oberhergheim/ditto   Texas

8:3121   14 Sep 1846
RUPPE, Andre Appolinaire, age 62, day laborer
--/Thann   New York

8:3122   14 Sep 1846
FUCHS, Martin, age 28, laborer; with brother
Oberhergheim/ditto   Texas

8:3125   16 Sep 1846
BOURGUIN, Francois, age 27, sawyer; with wife & 2
   children
Grosne/Mulhausen   Texas

8:3126   16 Sep 1846
BARTZ, Barbe, age 22, factory worker
Lemberg, Moselle/Mulhausen   Texas

8:3127   16 Sep 1846
HERMANN, Jean Gregoire, age 25, spinner
Reichshoffen, Bas-Rhin/Mulhausen?   Texas

8:3129   17 Sep 1846
HEIMBRECHT? [HUSUBRECHT?], Joseph, age 37, --?; with
   wife & 1 child
Oderen/Mulhausen   Texas

8:3130   17 Sep 1846
BACHMANN, Sebastien, age 53, day laborer
Rouffach/Biltzheim   Texas

8:3131   17 Sep 1846
BITTERLIN, Pierre Paul, age 47, farmer
Wettolsheim/Oberhergheim   Texas

8:3132   17 Sep 1846
WAGNER, Xavier, age 41, cooper; with wife
Rouffach/ditto   Texas

8:3134   17 Sep 1846
SCHAUB, Joseph, age 42, day laborer; with wife & mo-
   ther
Rixheim/ditto   Texas

18

8:3135   17 Sep 1846
KLUR, Charles, age 17, vine grower
Ingersheim/ditto   New York

8:3137   17 Sep 1846
HAGENMULLER? [HAGEMUELLER?], Jean, age 28, saddler
Oberhergheim/ditto   Texas

8:3139   19 Sep 1846
JABLER? [GABLER?], Jean, age 5, --?
Meurwiller? [Munwiller?]/ditto   Texas

8:3140   19 Sep 1846
MEYER, Francoise, age 22, servant
Oberentzen/ditto   Texas

8:3141   19 Sep 1846
LINZENMEYER, Antoine, age 44, wheelwright
Colmar/ditto   Waterloo, America

8:3143   21 Sep 1846
NAEGELIN, Michel, age 37, farmer; with wife & 6 chil-
    dren
Hirtzfelden/ditto   Texas

8:3144   21 Sep 1846
STROSSER, Paul, age 33, farmer; with wife & 1 child
Hirtzfelden/ditto   Texas

8:3145   21 Sep 1846
STROSSER, Antoine, age 20, domestic
Hirtzfelden/ditto   Texas

8:3146   21 Sep 1846
FEST, Simon, age 19, domestic
Hirtzfelden/ditto   Texas

8:3147   21 Sep 1846
BIHL, Michel, age 50, day laborer; with daughter
Hirtzfelden/ditto   Texas

8:3148   21 Sep 1846
TRIGLER? [CRIGLER?], Barthelemie, age 21, tailor
Rueffenhart? [Bueffenhart?]/Hirtzfelden? Texas

8:3151   21 Sep 1846
HAMALLE, Jean Baptiste, age 27, --; with wife & child
Niffer/Grandvillars   Chicago

8:3152   21 Sep 1846
SINGRUEN? [LINGRUEN?], Joseph, age 45, day laborer
Battenheim/Rixheim   Texas

8:3155   21 Sep 1846
HARTMANN, Andre, age 44, carpenter
Kochendorf, Wuerttemberg/Martzwiller   New York

8:3158   23 Sep 1846
BIPPERT, Jacques, age 47, vine grower; with wife & 2
    children
Mittelwihr/Riquemont?   Texas

8:3162   23 Sep 1846
LOEW? Aloyse, age 19, baker
Ribeauville/ditto   New Orleans

8:3164   24 Sep 1846
MUNCH, Bernard, age 53, joiner
Marckolsheim/Hattstatt   Texas

8:3165   24 Sep 1846
BIHL, Joseph, age 30, carpenter; with wife & 2 chil-
    dren
--/Hirtzfelden   Texas

8:3166   24 Sep 1846
JECKER? [JETTER?], Joseph Jacques, age --, weaver;
    with wife & 3 children
Wattwiller/ditto   Caracas, Venezuela

8:3167   25 Sep 1846
ENDERLEN, Vincent, dit Sebastien, age 23, --?
Soppe-le-Bas/ditto   New York

8:3168   28 Sep 1846
GRILLOT, Francois Joseph, age 29m, --?; with wife
Mort-et-Vaugney/Grandvillers   New York

8:3174   29 Sep 1846
LEFEVRE, Hypolite, age 42, day laborer; with grand-
    son?
St.-Hypolite/Colmar   New York

8:3178   01 Oct 1846
SCHWAB, Paul, age 54, farmer; with wife
Mauspach/ditto   New York

8:3179   01 Oct 1846
KAUFFMANN, Chretien, age 32, day laborer; with wife &
    7 children
Hallen, Switzerland/Blotzheim   Lottercantz?, America

8:3180   01 Oct 1846
SCHMERBES?, Joseph, age 29 day laborer; with wife
--/Hochstatt   Texas

8:3181   01 Oct 1846
PFISTER, Joseph, age 46, weaver
Traubach-le-Bas/ditto   New York

8:3182   01 Oct 1846
MATT, Jean, age 36, carpenter; with wife & 5 children
Fischerbach, Baden/Logelbach, Colmar
                                  St. Louis, America

8:3184   01 Oct 1846
RELISCHUNG? [REBISCHUNG?], Nicolas, age --, day
    laborer
Mitzach/ditto   Texas

8:3186   03 Oct 1846
PETER, Marie Anne, age 31, dressmaker
Malmerspach/ditto   Texas

8:3187   03 Oct 1846
HEYLANDT, Louis, age 61, --?; with wife & grandson
--/Hunawihr   New York

8:3189   05 Oct 1846
ERNST, Christe, age 23, weaver; with sister?
Boron/ditto   New York

8:3190   05 Oct 1846
CAYOT, Francois, age 40, blacksmith; with wife & 5
    children
Bessoncourt/ditto   New York

8:3191   06 Oct 1846
WICKERSHEIM, Matthias, age 47, weaver; with sister
Ostheim/ditto   New York

8:3194   06 Oct 1846
GANGLER, Madelaine, widow of -- FREYBOURGER; with 5
    children
Rimbach/Traubach-le-Bas   New York

8:3195   06 Oct 1846
LIEBELIN, Joseph, age 31, day laborer; with wife
Chaux/ditto   New York

8:3196   06 Oct 1846
CHAPUIS, Ferdinand, age 36, farmer; with wife & 2?
    children
--/Chapelle-sous-Chaux   Ohio

8:3197   06 Oct 1846
CHAPUIS, Pierre Julien, age 39, farmer; with mother
--/Chapelle-sous-Chaux   Ohio

8:3199   09 Oct 1846
WETZEL, Jean, age 25, house painter
Munster/ditto   New York

8:3200   09 Oct 1846
WEBER, Frederic, age 21, glazier
Munster/ditto   New York

8:3203   09 Oct 1846
FORWENDEL, Joseph, age 30?, shoemaker
Durrenbach, Bas-Rhin/Ste.-Croix-aux-Mines   New York

8:3204   09 Oct 1846
ANIEL? [ANCEL?], Alexandre, age 21, shoemaker
Ste.-Croix-aux-Mines/ditto   New York

8:3210   12 Oct 1846
WICKERSHEIM, Jean, age 50, dyer; with 2 children
Ostheim/Riquewihr   Chicago

8:3211   12 Oct 1846
NEHR, Joseph, age 48, day laborer; with wife & son
St.-Amerin/Mitzach   Texas

8:3214   14 Oct 1846
ZERR, Jean Baptiste, age 43, weaver; with wife & 3
    children
Mittelwihr/ditto   Texas

8:3216   14 Oct 1846
SCHERRER, Joseph, age 68, farmer; with wife, 5 chil-
    dren, & mother-in-law
Wolfersdorff/ditto   New York

8:3217   14 Oct 1846
MATHIEU, Louise, age 18, factory worker
Ste.-Croix-aux-Mines/ditto   St. Louis, America

8:3218   15 Oct 1846
WOLF, Barbe, age 27, servant
Seltz, Bas-Rhin/Mulhausen   New York

8:3219   15 Oct 1846
HUG, Ferdinand, age 20, commercial agent
Mulhausen/ditto   New York

8:3221   16 Oct 1846
LITIGUE, Marie Therese, age 26, cotton printer
Ste.-Croix-aux-Mines/ditto   St. Louis, America

8:3222   16 Oct 1846
SCHEURER, Francois, age 30, quarryman; with wife & 1?
    child
Ste.-Croix-aux-Mines/ditto   St. Louis, America

8:3223   16 Oct 1846
GRUBER, Joseph, age 26, factory worker; with wife & 1
    child
Ste.-Croix-aux-Mines/ditto   St. Louis, America

8:3225   17 Oct 1846
AMANN, Seraphim, age 36, weaver; with wife & 1 child
--/Hagenthal-le-Bas   Milwaukee

8:3229   20 Oct 1846
STEFFANY, Francois, age 44?, factory worker; with
    wife & 1 child
Thann/ditto   New York

8:3232   20 Oct 1846
SOMMER, Chretien, age 19, weaver
Ste.-Marie-aux-Mines/Ribeauville New York

8:3234   22 Oct 1846
LIBRE, Prospere, age 28, farmer
Bessoncourt/ditto   New York

8:3235   22 Oct 1846
LENGELIN? [SENGELIN?], Jean, age 21, tailor
Grentzingen/ditto   New York

8:3237   23 Oct 1846
SUISSE, Jean, age 20, farmer
Ste.-Marie-aux-Mines/Liepvre   New York

8:3238   23 Oct 1846
HESTIN, Joseph, age 29, farmer; with wife & 1 child
Allemand Rousbach? [Ronsbach?]/Liepvre   New Orleans

8:3240   23 Oct 1846
STRUESS?, Francois, age 29, factory worker; with wife
    & 2 children, sister-in-law & mother-in-law
Neuwiller, Bas-Rhin/Mulhausen   New York

8:3241   23 Oct 1846
WUST, Reine, age 30, factory worker
Schleithal, Bas-Rhin/Mulhausen   New York

8:3243   23 Oct 1846
SCHNEIDER, Nicolas, age 24, factory worker; with wife
    sister-in-law, & mother-in-law
Epping, Moselle/Mulhausen   New york

8:3244   24 Oct 1846
WEYMANN, Francois, age 20, metal worker
Vieux Thann/Thann   New York

8:3245   24 Oct 1846
RUDINGER, Joseph, age 49, farmer; with wife & 5 chil-
    dren
Heiteren/ditto   Texas

8:3247   26 Oct 1846
LEISY, Jean, age 26, businessman
Colmar/Mulhausen   New Orleans

8:3251   27 Oct 1846
MARTIN, Antoine, age 37, blacksmith; with wife & son
Retzwiller/ditto   New Orleans

8:3252   27 Oct 1846
LIEBELIN, Jacques, age 34, farmer; with wife & 4
    children
Chaux/ditto   New Orleans

8:3253   27 Oct 1846
HARTMANN, Jean Claude, age 56, tilemaker; with wife &
    11? children
Rougemont/ditto   Philadelphia

8:3254   27 Oct 1846
GOUSSET, Jean Baptiste, age 43, farmer; with wife & 7
    children
Rougemont/ditto   Philadelphia

8:3255   27 Oct 1846
PELTIER, Jacques, age 49, farmer
--/Chappelle-sous-Chaux   Ohio

8:3257   28 Oct 1846
JACQUOT, Jean Baptiste, age 37, farmer
Ste.-Croix-aux-Mines/ditto   ST. Louis, America

8:3260   29 Oct 1846
FREYBURGER, Paul? le juin? [younger?], age 33, farmer
    with wife & 3 children
Traubach-le-Bas/ditto   New York

8:3261   29 Oct 1846
BURGY, Nicolas, age 35, --?
Herrlisheim/Oberhergheim   Texas

8:3262   30 Oct 1846
SIMORINE?, Georges, age 23, tailor; with wife
Herrlisheim?/Retzwiller   New York

8:3266   31 Oct 1846
PRUD'HOMME, Louis Joseph Augustin Eduard, age 23,
    practitioner?; with servant
Wusselmann?, Bas-Rhin/Rouffach   U. S. A.

8:3269   02 Nov 1846
VIGNOS? [VIGNOR?], Jean Claude, age 30; farmer
Chavannes-les-Grand/ditto   New York

8:3271   03 Nov 1846
DECKERT, Benoit, age 51, blacksmith; with wife, 4
    children, & niece
Blodelsheim/ditto   Texas

8:3273   03 Nov 1846
MULLER, Pantaleon, age 21, carpenter
Mulhausen/Bourgfelden   New York

8:3275   05 Nov 1846
BICHLER? [BIEHLER?], Jean Baptiste, age 32, baker
Guebwiller/ditto   New York

8:3277   06 Nov 1846
MONNIER, Jean Pierre, age 49, landowner
Chevremont?/ditto   New York

8:3278   06 Nov 1846
HUGUENOT, Jean Pierre, age 24, domestic
Novillard/Bessoncourt   New York

8:3279   06 Nov 1846
L'HOMME, Nicolas, age 42, farmer; with wife & 6 chil-
    dren
Sermamagny/ditto   New York

8:3284   07 Nov 1846
PETREMENT, Emile, age 27, joiner
Ste.-Croix-aux-Mines/ditto   St. Louis, USA

8:3286   09 Nov 1846
JOURDAIN, Michel, age 31, stonecutter; with wife & 3
    children
Offemont/ditto   New York

8:3290   10 Nov 1846
COURTOT, Francois, age 20, farmer
Andelmans?/ditto   New York

8:3291   10 Nov 1846
PEUGUET, Francois, age 24, stonecutter
Offemont/ditto   New York

8:3292   10 Nov 1846
PEUGUET, Pierre, age 20, stonecutter
Offemont/ditto   New York

8:3293   10 Nov 1846
COURTOT, Joseph, age 20, carpenter
Levenaux?/ditto   New York

8:3294   11 Nov 1846
TRAITELEUR, Desire, age 27, shoemaker
Offemont/ditto   New York

8:3294   11 Nov 1846
HOTZ, Etienne*
*This name marked out and replaced by TRAITELEUR, De-
sire above.

8:3296   11 Nov 1846
HUFF, Antoine, age 48, day laborer
Friessen/ditto   New York

8:3301   14 Nov 1846
NIEFERGOLD, Jean, age 27, day laborer
Durmenach?/ditto   New York

8:3304   14 Nov 1846
VIGNOS? [VIGNOR?[, Denis, age 28, factory worker
Chavannes-le-Grands/Mulhausen   New York

8:3308   19 Nov 1846
GRUSSI?, Jacques, age 27, day laborer; with wife & 2
    children
Rostey, Bas-Rhin/Guebwiller   New York

8:3314   25 Nov 1846
MULLER, Meinrad, age 26, day laborer
Strueth/ditto   Philadelphia

8:3323   03 Dec 1846
BURGER, Louis, age 28, day laborer
--/Wittelsheim   Philadelphia

8:3331   05 Dec 1846
ANDRE, Pierre, age 33, --?; with wife & 1 child
Ste.-Croix-aux-Mines/ditto   St. Louis, America

8:3332   05 Dec 1846
MATHIEU, Jean Pierre, age 36, --?; with wife & 2
    children
Ste.-Marie-aux-Mines/ditto   St. Louis, America

8:3335   09 Dec 1846
CUYOT, Jean Claude, age 51, farmer
Bessoncourt/ditto   New York

8:3336   10 Dec 1846
GUILLAUMEY, Celestin, age 18, joiner
Sermamagney/ditto   St. Louis, America

8:3340   11 Dec 1846
LEGAISSE?, Alexandre, age 44, weaver; with wife & 5
    children
Thannenkirch/ditto   Chicago

8:3342   14 Dec 1846
LIROT? [SIROT?], Maximin, age 22, student
Thannenkirch/ditto   Chicago

8:3344   14 Dec 1846
SCHNEIDER, Joseph, age 30, day laborer; with brother
    Georges
Bollwiller/Wittelsheim   Philadelphia

8:3354   18 Dec 1846
RICHERT, Jean Thiebaud, age 20, shoemaker
Fuelleren/ditto   Dover, America

8:3355   18 Dec 1846
SCHMITT, Joseph, age 27, baker
Fuelleren?/ditto   Dover, America

8:3356   19 Dec 1846
FAHRNER, Francois Joseph, age 41, weaver; with wife &
    4? children
Baldenheim, Bas-Rhin/Ste.-Croix-aux-Mines
                       St. Louis, America

8:3357   21 Dec 1846
WALCH, Louis, age 31, weaver; with wife & 1 child
St.-Amarin/ditto   New York

8:3363   23 Dec 1846
KOEGLER, Etienne, age 49, mason; with wife & 3 chil-
    dren
Fulleren? [Falleren?]/ditto   Dover, America

8:3365   24 Dec 1846
MEYER, Etienne, age 40, mason; with wife & --? chil-
    dren
Fulleren/ditto   Dover, America

8:3366   24 Dec 1846
GUNDY?, Joseph, age 48, shepherd; with wife
Fulleren/ditto   Dover, America

8:3367   24 Dec 1846
GUNDY, Sebastien, age 40, tilemaker; with wife & 8
   children
Fulleren/ditto   Dover, America

8:3368   24 Dec 1846
GISSINGER, Antoine, age 38, mason
--/Carspach   New York

8:3370   26 Dec 1846
SCHMITT, Jean, age 35, farmer
--/Hindlingen   New York

8:3376   30 Dec 1846
HASSENFRATZ, --, age 23, sawyer; with wife
Reichshoffen, Bas-Rhin/Guebwiller   New York

8:3378   30 Dec 1846
LOUIS, Frantz, age 29, farmer
Bourogne/ditto   New York

8:3380   02 Jan 1847
DROZ, Jean Pierre, age 64, farmer; with wife, son, &
   nephew
Chaux/ditto   New Orleans

8:3383   02 Jan 1847
DEUX? [DEUR?], Jean Pierre, age 22, farmer
Grandvillars/ditto   New York

8:3388   11 Jan 1847
HOFFERT, Jacques, age 21, saddler
Muntzenheim/ditto   New York

8:3389   11 Jan 1847
KLOETZLEN, Joseph, age 40, day laborer; with wife & 2
   children
Strueth/ditto   New York

8:3390   13 Jan 1847
GIRLOT? [KIRLOT?], Francois, age 35, farmer
Plancher-les-Bas, Haute Saone/Argiesaur?   New York

8:3393   16 Jan 1847
ENDERLEN, Joseph, age 60, day laborer; with wife,
   sister?, & 3 children
Strueth/ditto   New York

8:3396   18 Jan 1847
PHILIPPE, Thiebaut, age 32, farmer
Friessen/ditto   New York

8:3397   18 Jan 1847
LENTZ, Marie Anne, age 18, day laborer
--/Brechaumont   New York

8:3403   23 Jan 1847
STUCKY, Jacques, age 25, laborer?
Altkirch/ditto   New York

8:3404   25 Jan 1847
KIENE, Jean, age 45, farmer; with wife & 3? children
Uberkummen/ditto   New York

8:3405   25 Jan 1847
CUISINIER, Antoine, age 46, joiner; with wife & 3
   children
Vellescot/ditto   New York

8:3406   25 Jan 1847
MAIGRAT? [MAIGROT?], Francois, age 24, --?
Boron/ditto   New York

8:3407   25 Jan 1847
HEMELEN, Francois Joseph, age 31, farmer
Uberkummen/ditto   New York

8:3408   25 Jan 1847
KIENE, Andre, age 25, carpenter
Uberkummen/ditto   New York

8:3410   26 Jan 1847
KLOPFENSTEIN, Charles, age 45, farmer; with wife & 7?
   children
--/Belfort   New York

8:3411   27 Jan 1847
PAULIN, Stanislas, age 44, weaver; with father?, wife
   & 6? children
Moosch/Remagny   New York

8:3412   27 Jan 1847
COUVET, Francois, age 19, pastry cook
Ferrette/ditto   New York

8:3422   29 Jan 1847
FUCHS, Catherine, age 32, factory worker
Mulhausen/ditto   St. Louis, America

8:3425   30 Jan 1847
BUBSER? [BABSER?], Jean, age 28, shoemaker
Retzwiller/ditto   New Orleans

8:3426   30 Jan 1846
GROSJEAN, Joseph Nicolas, age 25, farmer
Montreux vieux?/ditto   New York

8:3427   30 Jan 1847
FLOTAT, Jean Pierre, age 27, farmer
Montreux vieux?/ditto   New York

8:3428   30 Jan 1847
GUITTARD? [GUILLARD?], Marie Catherine, age 22, far-
   mer
Montreux vieux?/ditto   New York

8:3429   30 Jan 1847
PREVOT, Marie Anne, age 59, farmer; with 2 children
--/Chaux   New Orleans

8:3432   01 Feb 1847
KOEGLER, Joseph, age 27, laborer?
--/Altenach   New Orleans

8:3435   02 Feb 1847
DURACHER, Barnabe, age 39, barber; with wife & 3
    children
Ste.-Marie-aux-Mines/ditto   New Orleans

8:3441   04 Feb 1847
GUITTARD, Francois Joseph, age 19, traveling salesman
Montreux-Vieux/Belfort   New York

8:3442   05 Feb 1847
PREVOT, Jean Louis, age 36, farmer; with wife & 2
    children
Chaux/ditto   New Orleans

8:3443   05 Feb 1847
BRIGUELEUR, Francois Xavier, age 23, farmer
Chaux/ditto   New Orleans

8:3444   05 Feb 1847
CHAPUIS, Thiebaud, age 55, farmer; with wife & 2
    children
--/Sermamagny   New Orleans

8:3446   06 Feb 1847
ORRIEZ, Francois, age 28, farmer; with wife, mother,
    & sister
Sermamagny/ditto   New Orleans

8:3447   09 Feb 1847
DELACROIX, Jean, age 28, cabinetmaker
Leymen/Levoncourt   New York

8:3448   09 Feb 1847
GAST, Joseph Antoine, age 36, sawyer; with wife & 3
    children
Ligsdorff/ditto   New York

8:3449   09 Feb 1847
HINGUE, Marie Therese, age 56; with 4 children
--/Lachapelle-sur-Chaux   Ohio

8:3450   09 Feb 1847
MARIE, Francois Xavier, age 28, farmer
Chaux/ditto   New Orleans

8:3452   10 Feb 1847
MUELLER? [MULLER?], Jean Baptiste, age 19, employee
    of --? --?
Ferrette/Altkirch   New York

8:3455   12 Feb 1847
CRAVE, Jean Baptiste, age 19, farmer
St.-Germain/ditto   New York

8:3463   15 Feb 1847
TSCHIRHART, Augustin, age 22, day laborer
Roderen/ditto   Baltimore

8:3464   15 Feb 1847
BROYEZ, Francois, age 25, farmer; with wife & 6?
    children
Recouvrance/ditto   New York

8:3465   15 Feb 1847
KEMPF, Jean, age 23, farmer
Altenach/ditto   New Orleans

8:3466   17 Feb 1847
DELAET, Jean Pierre, age 38, farmer; with wife & 1
    child
--/Grosne   New York

8:3467   17 Feb 1847
HESS, Joseph, age 22, baker
Roderen/ditto   Baltimore

8:3471   17 Feb 1847
SCHMITT, Andre, age --, --?
Illhaeusern/ditto   New York

8:3472   17 Feb 1847
BIEHLMANN, Michel, age 34, landowner
Hunawihr/ditto   New York

8:3473   17 Feb 1847
BOGEN, Gangolf, age 30, cooper
Bennwihr?/Huntzheim   New York

8:3475   18 Feb 1847
BOUCHEZ, Francois, age 35, farmer; with wife
Salbert/ditto   New Orleans

8:3476   18 Feb 1847
JARDON, Jean Claude, age 42, farmer; with wife & 9?
    children
Salbert/ditto   New Orleans

8:3478   18 Feb 1847
BOUCHEZ, Alexis, age 68, farmer; with wife & grandson
Salbert/ditto   New Orleans

8:3481   20 Feb 1847
SCHIGAND, Guillaume, age 25, day laborer
Durmenach/ditto   New York

8:3482   20 Feb 1847
HABERSTOCK, Francois Joseph, age 49, gardener; with
    niece
illegible/Philadelphia   Philadelphia

8:3483   20 Feb 1847
REBER, Joseph, age 20, laborer
Uffheim,/ditto   New York

8:3484   20 Feb 1847
FORSTER, Louis, age 20, weaver
Ferrette/ditto   New York

8:3485   20 Feb 1847
FISCHER, Thiebaud, age 25, weaver
Hindlingen/ditto   New York

8:3486   22 Feb 1847
SCHMITT, Joseph, age 62, carpenter; with wife & 3
    children
--/Jonchery   New York

9:0001   22 Feb 1847
MOUILLESEAUX, Marie, age 25, dressmaker
Andelnans/ditto   New York

9:0002   22 Feb 1847
PECHIN, Celestin, age 22, tailor
--/Jonchery   New York

9:0003   22 Feb 1847
DUBORONSKI, Etienne, age 55, mason; with wife & 4
    daughters
--/Jonchery   New York

9:0005   24 Feb 1847
FLEURY, Jean Pierre, age 46, farmer; with wife, 4
    children, & nephew
Faverois/Vellescot   New York

9:0006   25 Feb 1847
SCHAEFFER, Sebastien, age 36, day laborer
Oberhergheim/ditto   Philadelphia

9:0009   01 Mar 1847
MENAGER, Maurice, age 40, day laborer
Belfort/Jonchery   New York

9:0011   02 Mar 1847
RAPP, Andre, age 37, farmer; with wife, 2 children, &
    brother
Sondersdorff/ditto   New York

9:0012   02 Mar 1847
SCHALTENBRAND, Leopold, age 19, dyer
--/Pfetterhausen   New York

9:0013   02 Mar 1847
DATTLER, Francois Joseph, age 19, tilemaker
Pfetterhausen/ditto   New York

9:0014   02 Mar 1847
GSCHWIND, Dominique, age 20, nailmaker
Pfetterhausen/ditto   New York

9:0015   02 Mar 1847
JAEGLIN, Meinrad, age 19, tilemaker
Pfetterhausen/ditto   New York

9:0016   02 Mar 1847
GASSET, Anotine, age 19, mason
Pfetterhausen/ditto   New York

9:0017   02 Mar 1847
EHLINGER, Jacques, age 24, ironworker
Moosch/bitschwiller   New York

9:0018   02 Mar 1847
VETTER, Martin, age 19, day laborer
Sondersdorff/ditto   New York

9:0019   02 Mar 1847
DELAET, Joseph, Junior, age 20, farmer
Vellescot/ditto   New York

9:0020   02 Mar 1847
MOINE, Pierre --?, age 65, day laborer; with 2 sons
Boron/ditto   New York

9:0021   02 Mar 1847
REDELLE, Francois Alexandre, age 35, farmer
Grandvillars/ditto   New York

9:0022   02 Mar 1847
DELIMSCH?, Jean Adam, age 30, laborer
--/Pfetterhausen   New York

9:0023   02 Mar 1847
HEYER, Joseph Antoine, age 35, farmer; with wife & 5
    children
--/Pfetterhausen   New York

9:0027   04 Mar 1847
DUPRE, Francois, age 26, day laborer
--/Roppe   New York

9:0028   04 Mar 1847
LIBRE, Alexandre, age 28?, day laborer; with wife & 3
    children
--/Roppe   New York

9:0029   04 Mar 1847
EGLE, Jacques, age 36, landowner; with wife, 2 bro-
    thers, & maid
Erkholsheim?, Bas-Rhin/Wintzenheim   New York

9:0032   05 Mar 1847
ROSIET, Jean Pierre, age 41, day laborer; with wife &
    2 children
Vetrigne/ditto   New York

9:0034   06 Mar 1847
METROT? [METROL?], Georges, age 30, day laborer
--/Jonchery   New York

9:0035   06 Mar 1847
FISCHER, Joseph, age 37, carpenter; with wife & 2
    children
--/Jonchery   New York

9:0036   06 Mar 1847
PRONEZ? [PRENEZ?], Sebastien, age 19, wooden shoe-
    maker
Jonchery/ditto   New York

9:0037   06 Mar 1847
PRONGUE?, Marie, age 36, day laborer
Jonchery/ditto   New York

9:0039   08 Mar 1847
FERAND? [FERARD?], Marie Francoise, age 19, tailor
--/Foussemagne   New York

9:0040   08 Mar 1847
GRISEZ, Ferriol?, age 36, day laborer; with wife & 4
    children
Plancher, Haute-Saone/Andelnans   New Orleans

9:0041   08 Mar 1847
GRISEZ, Claude Paschal?, age 63, day laborer; with
    wife?
--/Andelnans   New Orleans

9:0043   08 Mar 1847
RIVIERE, Francois, age 36, day laborer; with wife &
    3 children
Cermarancher?, Seine-et-Loire/Andelnans   New York

9:0047   09 Mar 1847
BARBIES? [BARBIER?], Jacques, age 37, farmer; with
    wife & 2 children
--/Grosne   New York

9:0048   10 Mar 1847
BRONNER?, Frederic, age 29, baker; with wife
Mulhausen/ditto   New York

9:0050   10 Mar 1847
SIMENDINGER, Joseph, age 22, carpenter
Pfetterhausen/ditto   New York

9:0053   12 Mar 1847
DONZE, Denis, age 46?, farmer; with wife & 2 children
--/Montroux-Chateau   New York

9:0054   12 Mar 1847
BLONDE, Joseph, Junior?, age 19, farmer; with sister?
    Emilien?
Brechaumont/ditto   New York

9:0055   12 Mar 1847
BLONDE, Nicolas, age 42?, farmer; with wife, 5 chil-
    dren, & maid
Brechaumont/ditto   New York

9:0056   12 Mar 1847
BIHL, Marguerite, age 20, farmer
Brechaumont/ditto   New York

9:0057   12 Mar 1847
CLER, Xavier, age 18, farmer
Brechaumont/ditto   New York

9:0058   12 Mar 1847
MEYER, Jean, age 27, woodturner
Ostheim/ditto   New York

9:0059   12 Mar 1847
DURLIOT, Sebastien, age 37, day laborer
Brechaumont/ditto   New York

9:0060   12 Mar 1847
WEISS, Catherine, age 21, day laborer
Brechaumont/ditto   New York

9:0065   15 Mar 1847
GRAF, Jean, age 44, factory worker; with wife
Carspach/ditto   New York

9:0067   15 Mar 1847
DIETRICH, Simon, age 45, shoemaker; with wife & 8
    children
--/Faverois   New Orleans

9:0069   15 Mar 1847
HEINZ, Jacques, age 24, factory worker
Scheibenhard, Rhenish Bavaria/Mulhouse   New York

9:0073   17 Mar 1847
MAGER, Melchior, age 32, --?
Benningen, Wuerttemberg/Ste.-Marie-aux-Mines New York

9:0074   17 Mar 1847
HANAUER, Jacques, age 24, vine grower
Hunawihr/ditto   New York

9:0075   17 Mar 1847
OBERST, Jean, age 35, day laborer
Seppois-le-Haut/ditto   New York

9:0076   17 Mar 1847
BITSCH, Nicolas, age 31, weaver
Guevenatten/ditto   New York

9:0077   17 Mar 1847
KIENE, Antoine, age 38, farmer
Uberkummen/Courtelevant   New York

9:0080   18 Mar 1847
BURNER, Joseph, age 22, saddler
Brunstatt/ditto   New York

9:0081   18 Mar 1847
KELLER, Louis, age 24, baker
Brunstatt/ditto   New York

9:0082   18 Mar 1847
MATOUILLET, Francois, age 48, farmer; with wife &
    mother
Sebetan? [Lebetan?]/ditto   New York

9:0083   18 Mar 1847
GUERRINGE, Bernard, age 48, farmer; with wife & 5
    children
Sebetan? [Lebetan?]/ditto   New York

9:0085   19 Mar 1847
TONDRE, George, age 45, blacksmith; with wife & 2
    children
Eteimbes/ditto   New York

9:0086   19 Mar 1847
MOURRE? [MOURNE?], Anne, age 28, --; with 8? children
Vezeles/Belfort   New Orleans

9:0087   19 Mar 1847
PIQUEREZ, Francois, age 34, day laborer; with wife &
    2? children
Andelnans/Belfort?   New Orleans

9:0088   19 Mar 1847
VOILANT, Louis, age 34, day laborer; with wife & 2
    children
Belfort/ditto   New York

9:0098   20 Mar 1847
BERNARD, Madeleine, age 23, no profession
Kayserberg/Hunawihr   New York

9:0092   22 Mar 1847
MEISTER, Francois Xavier, age 25, farmer
--/Bisel   New York

9:0096   22 Mar 1847
AMANN, Jean, Jr., age 21, horticulturist
Ste.-Marie-aux-Mines/ditto   New York

9:0097   22 Mar 1847
EHRET, Francois, age 46, nailmaker
Massevaux/ditto   New York

9:0098   22 Mar 1847
FURLINDER, Charles, age 30, tailor; with wife, 2
    children, brother-in-law, & sister-in-law
Massevaux/ditto   New York

9:0102   24 Mar 1847
REY, Thiebaud, age 25, joiner
--/Pfetterhausen   New York

9:0103   25 Mar 1847
WOHLSCHLAG, Andre, age 39, vine grower; with wife & 1
    child
Gueberswihr? [Gueberschwihr?]/Herrlesheim   New York

9:0104   25 Mar 1847
SCHNEBELIN, Antoine, age 44, blacksmith; with wife &
    6 children
Buntzenheim/ditto   New York

9:0105   25 Mar 1847
KUEN, Mathias, age 27?, vine grower; with wife & 2
    children
Mulhausen/ditto   New York

9:0109   25 Mar 1847
BENDELE, Martin, age 69, vine grower
Herrlisheim/ditto   New York

9:0110   25 Mar 1847
FRICK, Michel, age 38, vine grower; with wife & 5
    children
Herrlisheim/ditto   New York

9:0113   25 Mar 1847
GOUTTERMANN, Jean Crisostome, age 46, master orti-
    fuge?; with wife, 3 children, sister-in-law & 2
    children, & maid?
Troyes, Aube/Ste./-Marie-aux-Mines   New Orleans

9:0114   26 Mar 1847
SCHIRMES? [SCHIRMER?], Louis, age 38, tailor
Niedersteinbrunn/ditto   New York

9:0115   26 Mar 1847
FEUTE?, Marguerite, widow of -- FINSTERBACH, age 42;
    with 5 children
Offemont/Danjoutin   New York

9:0121   27 Mar 1847
BRUNNER, Francois Joseph, age 25, locksmith; with
    wife & 3 children
Fessenheim/Colmar   New York

9:0123   27 Mar 1847
FELLMANN? [FOLLMANN?], Joseph, age 23, saddler
Herrlisheim/ditto   New York

9:0124   29 Mar 1847
WEINMANN, Francois Joseph, age 39, waiter?; with wife
    & 2 children
--/Thann   New York

9:0125   29 Mar 1847
BEON, Jean Pierre, age 41, locksmith; with wife &
    daughter
Alexandrief, Piemont/ditto   New York

9:0126   29 Mar 1847
WAAG, Louis, age 37, locksmith; with wife & 3 chil-
    dren
Andlau, Bas-Rhin/ditto   New York

9:0127   29 Mar 1847
MAITRE, Joseph, age 39, factory worker; with wife & 2
    children
Ebauviller, Switzerland/Sentheim   New York

9:0128   29 Mar 1847
HUSSER, Jacques, age 27, day laborer
Muntzenheim/ditto   New York

9:0132   30 Mar 1847
KINNENBERG? [KIRMENBERGER?], Jean Georges, age 25,
    carpenter
Pothran?, Baden/Guebwiller   New York

9:0133   30 Mar 1847
COCK? Antoine, age 28, carpenter
Vieux-Brisach/ditto   New York

9:0134   30 Mar 1847
SCHOENENBERGER, Joseph Antoine, age 60, --?; with
    wife & 1 child
Butzenschwill?, Switzerland/St.-Louis   Cincinnati

9:0135   30 Mar 1847
HECK, Catherine, age 25; with sister
Le Puix [Lepuix]/ditto   New York

9:0136   30 Mar 1847
JOLIER, Pierre Joseph, age 38, --; with wife & 4?
    children
Le Puix [Lepuix]/ditto   New York

9:0137   30 Mar 1847
WALKRE, Joseph, age 31, --
Le Puix [Lepuix]/ditto   New York

9:0138   30 Mar 1847
DUPREZ, Pierre, age 24, farmer
--/Lebetain   New York

9:0139   30 Mar 1847
DUPREZ, Francois, age 22, --
--/Lebetain   New York

9:0143   31 Mar 1847
SEILLER, Jean, age 41, joiner; with wife & 3 children
Massevaux/ditto   New York

9:0144   31 Mar 1847
SCHABTAG, Catherine, age 24, dressmaker; with child
St.-Die/Ste.Marie-aux-Mines   New Orleans

9:0146   31 Mar 1847
JAEGER, Joseph Mathieu, age 36, --; with wife & 2
    children
Massevaux/Mortzwiller   New York

9:0147   01 Apr 1847
GUTZWILLER, Jean Aloyse, age 30, tailor
Biederthal/ditto   New York

9:0148   01 Apr 1847
WEPFER, Joseph, age 23, work master?
Thann/ditto   New York

9:0149   01 Apr 1847
FREY, Joseph, age 21, day laborer
Betzwiller/Dannemarie   New York

9:0150   01 Apr 1847
SEILLER, Jean Baptiste, age 23, --?
Massevaux/ditto   New York

9:0155   01 Apr 1847
LAGEZ, Melchior, age 48, farmer; with wife & 3 chil-
    dren
Sermamagny/ditto   New Orleans

9:0157   02 Apr 1847
BOHL, Jean, age 35, cooper
Massevaux/ditto   New York

9:0158   02 Apr 1847
FIAT, Charles, age 27, locksmith
Massevaux/ditto   New York

9:0159   02 Apr 1847
RICHARD, Simon, age 30, day laborer; with wife & 2
    children
--/Bretagne   New York

9:0160   02 Apr 1847
WIRTH, Antoine, age 33, tailor
Massevaux/ditto   New York

9:0161   03 Apr 1847
STENG, --, widow, nee TREJEAN, age 46; with son
--/Eteimbes   New York

9:0165   06 Apr 1847
SEILLER, Jean, age 44, day laborer
Massevaux? [or Masse-Vieux]/ditto   New York

9:0166   06 Apr 1847
LAIBE, Jean Dione?, age 33, joiner
Faveroil? [Faverois?]/ditto   New York

9:0167   06 Apr 1847
HENCKY, Jean, age 33, baker; with family
Riquewihr/ditto   New York

9:0169   06 Apr 1847
ROUECHE, Francois, age 24, landowner
Angeot/ditto   New York

9:0171   06 Apr 1847
GUTZWILLER, Xavier, age 32, --? --?
Biederthal/ditto   New York

9:0172   06 Apr 1847
FROEHLY, Joseph, age 48, wagoner; with family
Vieux-Ferrette/ditto   New York

9:0173   06 Apr 1847
RICHARD, Francois, age 29, woodturner; with sister &
   her children
--/Faveroix   New Orleans

9:0174   07 Apr 1847
FROEHLY, Ursule, widow of -- SCHICKLER, age 51; with
   2 sons, sister, & servant
Vieux-Ferrette/ditto   New York

9:0175   07 Apr 1847
UMBDENSTOCK, Chretien, age 18, --
Mittelwihr/ditto   New York

9:0176   07 Apr 1847
MARSOT, Joseph, age 41, farmer; with wife & 2 chil-
   dren
--/Sermamagny   New Orleans

9:0178   08 Apr 1847
GUTHMANN, Francois Xavier, age 28, shoemaker
Fessenheim/ditto   New York

9:0179   08 Apr 1847
GINOT, Antoine, age 36, shoemaker?
Massevaux/ditto   New York

9:0180   08 Apr 1847
BIRRER, Jean Cornel, age 33, factory worker
Willer/Massevaux   New York

9:0182   08 Apr 1847
MEYER, Francois Joseph, age 19, farmer
Sondersdorff/ditto   New York

9:0183   08 Apr 1847
CHAVANNE, Maurice, age 40, farmer; with wife & 3
   children
--/St.-Dizier   New York

9:0184   09 Apr 1847
LABOUEBE?, Pierre Joseph, age 19, farmer
Lutrun? [Sutrun?]/Floremont   New Orleans

9:0188   09 Apr 1847
ULLMANN, Mathias, age 21, merchant
Durmenach/ditto   New Orleans

9:0189   09 Apr 1847
ALTENBACH, Etienne, age 47, farmer; with wife, 2
   children, & maid
Sondersdorff/ditto   New York

9:0190   09 Apr 1847
DEUS? [DEUR?], Francois, age 18, farmer
--/St.-Dizier   New Orleans

9:0191   09 Apr 1847
CLOR? [CLORS?], Anne Marie, age 26, farmer
--/Brechaumont   New York

9:0193   09 Apr 1847
STUDER? [HUDER?], Aime, age 31, shoemaker; with wife
   & sister-in-law
Oberbruk [Oberbruck]/Soppe-le-Haut   New Orleans

9:0194   09 Apr 1847
TSCHERHART, Nicolas, age 45, landowner; with wife, 4
   children, & maid
Soppe-le-Haut/ditto   New Orleans

9:0195   09 Apr 1847
RAETTICH, Francois Joseph, age 30, factory worker;
   with wife, 1 child, & brother-in-law
Staffelfelden/Thann   Pittsburgh

9:0199   10 Apr 1847
LOILLIER, Charles Joseph, age 19, --
Courcelles/ditto   New York

9:0200   10 Apr 1847
LINDER, Jean, age 30, carpenter
Niedermuespach/ditto   New York

9:0202   12 Apr 1847
HELLER, Henri, age 55, farmer; with wife & 4 children
Oberlesbach, Switzerland/Colmar   New York

9:0203   12 Apr 1847
BARBARAS? [BARBASAS?], Georges, age 42, weaver; with
   wife, 3 children, & sister
Ostheim/ditto   New York

9:0205   12 Apr 1847
HANS, David, age 46, day laborer; with wife, 7? chil-
   dren, & mother-in-law
Hunawihr/Ostheim   New York

9:0207   13 Apr 1847
GROSJEAN, Jean Baptiste, age 29, founderer; with bro-
   ther
Ste.-Marie-aux-Mines/ditto   New Orleans

9:0208   13 Apr 1847
EHRET, Antoine, age 39, locksmith; with wife
Massevaux/Vieux-Thann   New York

9:0209   13 Apr 1847
HERSCHBERGER, Georges, age 53, wheelwright; with wife
   & 3 children, daughter & [her] 2 children, --
   [other accompanying persons?]
Ostheim/ditto   New York

9:0210   13 Apr 1847
CHRISTEN, Jean Jacques, age 24, wheelwright
Balschwiller/ditto   New York

9:0211   13 Apr 1847
GERTHOFFER, Francois Joseph, age 32
--/Burnhaupt-le-Haut   New York

9:0212   13 Sep 1847
SPIESS, Francois Joseph, age 47, coppersmith
Ste.-Marie-aux-Mines/ditto   New Orleans

9:0214   13 Apr 1847
HEIM, Georges, Junior, age 29, saddler; with wife & 2
    children
Ostheim/ditto   New York

9:0215   13 Apr 1847
UMBDENSTOCK, Mathias, age 30, glazier
Ostheim/ditto   New York

9:0216   13 Apr 1847
KLEIN, Mathias, age 28, day laborer; with wife & 4
    children
Ostheim/ditto   New York

9:0217   13 Apr 1847
FROELICH, Catherine, age 20, day laborer; with sister
Ostheim/ditto   New York

9:0218   13 Apr 1847
KABIS, Joseph, age 31, factory worker; with 1 child &
    mother-in-law
Kaysersberg/ditto   New York

9:0219   13 Apr 1847
HINDERMANN, Jean Jacques, age 31, glazier; with wife
Herbourg?/ditto   New York

9:0220   13 Apr 1847
MAETHER? [MOETHER?], Jean de Louis, age 41, day la-
    borer
Ostheim/ditto   New York

9:0221   13 Apr 1847
VIELWEBER, David, age 67, cooper; with sons
Hunawihr/Jebsheim   New York

9:0222   14 Apr 1847
EICHER, Jacques, age 38, farmer; with wife? & child
Rougemont/Staffelfelden   Ohio

9:0223   14 Apr 1847
SIEFFERMANN? [LIEFFERMANN?], Laurent, age 27, coach-
    man?; with wife & 1 child
Willer, Bas-Rhin/Guebwiller?   New York

9:0226   15 Apr 1847
HIROT? [LIROT?[, Gregoire, age 25, cook
Thannenkirch/ditto   New York

9:0228   15 Apr 1847
KULSCH? [KIELSCH?], Antoine, age 54, factory worker;
    with wife & 4 children
Luxhausen, Bas-Rhin/Colmar   Pittsburgh

9:0231   16 Apr 1847
MOINAT, Catherine, age 24, --
--/St.-Dizier   New York

9:0233   17 Apr 1847
SEILLER, Francois Xavier, age 25, joiner
Soultz/Walbach   New York

9:0235   19 Apr 1847
RICHARD, Jacques, age 47, weaver; with wife & 6 chil-
    dren
Wolfersdorff/ditto   New York

9:0236   19 Apr 1847
ENDERLEN, Pierre, age 34, farmer
Soppe-le-Bas/Mortzwiller   New York

9:0237   19 Apr 1847
BIHLER, Apollinaire, age 53, day laborer; with wife
Bourbach-le-Bas/Sentheim   New York

9:0238   19 Apr 1847
THURING, Pierre, age 31, wheelwright; with wife & 4
    children
Belfort/ditto   New York

9:0239   19 Apr 1847
HORNER? [HORNES?], Jacques, age 28, baker
--/Wolfersdorff   New York

9:0240   19 Apr 1847
DELLUNG, Ignace, age 53, farmer
--/Wolfersdorff   New York

9:0243   21 Apr 1847
GERTHOFFER, Jean, age 61, weaver; with wife & 5 chil-
    dren
--/Burnhaupt-le-Haut   New York

9:0244   21 Apr 1847
GOMMENGINGER?, Joseph Louis, age 46, weaver; with
    wife & 1 child
Andlau, Bas-Rhin/--   New York

9:0245   21 Apr 1847
MEYER, Francois Joseph, age 39, weaver; with wife & 4
    children
--/Burnhaupt-le-Haut   New York

9:0246   21 Apr 1847
TERNE, Bernard, age 19, joiner
Guebwiller/ditto   New York

9:0247   21 Apr 1847
JOUN?, Claude Didier, [no age given], mason
Bonhomme?/ditto   New York

9:0251   21 Apr 1847
SCHULER, Henri, age 63, weaver; with wife & daughter,
   [illegible] & 2 children
--/Burnhaupt-le-Haut   New York

9:0254   22 Apr 1847
WACKER, Antoine, age 52, farmer
Bourwiller/ditto   New York

9:0255   22 Apr 1847
FOLTZ, Joseph, age 51, farmer
Bourwiller/ditto   New York

9:0257   22 Apr 1847
BOUCHEZ, Jacques Etienne, age 38, farmer
Salbert?/ditto   New Orleans

9:0260   24 Apr 1847
RICHARDT, Joseph, age 22, tailor
Bouxwiller/ditto   New York

9:0263   24 Apr 1847
ROGENMUSER, Joseph, age 25, barber
Altkirch/ditto   New York

9:0264   26 Apr 1847
GOETZ, Georges Joseph, age 35, vine grower; wtih wife
   & 2 children
--/Ribeauville   New York

9:0265   26 Apr 1847
EHRET, Antoine, age 47, farmer; with wife, 6? chil-
   dren, & 2 grandchildren
Rammersmatt/Bourbach-le-Bas   New York

9:0266   26 Apr 1847
GETSCHY, Dominique, age 22, shoemaker
Steinsultz?/ditto   New York

9:0267   26 Apr 1847
KAEPPELIN, Aime, Antoine, age 28, [illegible]
Mulhausen/ditto   New York

9:0269   26 Apr 1847
BUEHER? [BUCHER?], Jean Thiebaut, age 26, --
Schweighausen/ditto   New York

9:0270   26 Apr 1847
LEMAIRE, Joseph, age 30, sawyer; with wife & 1 child
Pexonne, Meurthe/Mulhouse   New York

9:0278   28 Apr 1847
WITT, Antoine, age 35, farmer
Bisel/ditto   New York

9:0279   28 Apr 1847
JUDLIN, Joseph, age 34, farmer
hann/ditto   New York

9:0282   29 Apr 1847
VOGELWEIDT, Seraphim, age 46, day laborer
Bisel/ditto   New York

9:0283   29 Apr 1847
BERGER, Francois Antoine?, age 30, farmer
Bisel/ditto   New York

9:0284   29 Apr 1847
THOMAS, Jean Pierre, age 37, factory worker; with
   wife, 4 children, & sister-in-law
Pfastadt/ditto   St. Louis de Potosi, America
                                        [Mexico]

9:0296   04 May 1847
ALBITZ, George, 153 23, joiner
Urschenheim? [Arschenheim?]/ditto New York

9:0298   05 May 1847
FEBER, Morand, age 40, farmer; with wife & 6 children
St.-Ulrich/ditto   New York

9:0306   08 May 1847
HINTZY, Gaspard Mathias, age 28, carpenter
Colmar/ditto   New York

9:0308   08 May 1847
FISCHER, Georges, age 55, farmer; with wife, 8? chil-
   dren, --?, & 2 granddaughters
Kuenheim?/ditto   New York

9:0310   10 May 1847
ROSIER, Jean Baptiste, age 28, --
Offemont/ditto   New York

9:0313   10 May 1847
ROSIER, Etienne, age 25, --
Offemont/ditto   New York

9:0314   10 May 1847
BAUME, Jacques, age 22, --
Offemont/ditto   New York

9:0323   14 May 1847
FLEURY, Marie, age 26, --
Lepuix/ditto   New York

9:0324   14 May 1847
HEINMELIN? [HEMMELIN?], Joseph Wendelin, age 31,
   joiner
Balschwiller/ditto   New York

9:0325   14 May 1847
MAURER?, Fortune, age 36, day laborer; with wife & 2
   children
St.-Ulrich/ditto   New York

9:0326   14 May 1847
FEBER, Morand, son of Morand, age 32, day laborer
St.-Ulrich/ditto   New York

9:0327   14 May 1847
KAEHLER, Dida--? [Didier?], age 29, joiner
Balschwiller/ditto   New York

9:0329   14 May 1847
SCHALLER, Georges, age 42, wheelwright; wife wife & 1
    child
Michelbach, Switzerland?/ditto   New York

9:0335   15 May 1847
WALTER, Andre, age 20, wheelwright
Gebsheim/ditto   New York

9:0339   15 May 1847
BRAUN?, Jacques, age 21, --
Durrenentzen/ditto   Chicago

9:0340   17 May 1847
AEUNIUEX?, Antoine, age 27, farmer; with wife
--/Gorth?   New York

9:0341   17 May 1847
TEGUIGNOT? [PEGUIGNOT?, SEGUIGNOT?], Jean Baptiste,
    age 25, --?
Errevit?, Haute-Saone/ditto   New York

9:0344   17 May 1847
ANTOINE, Thiebaud, age 19, farmer
Chevremont/ditto   New York

9:0349   19 May 1847
CHRISTEN, Francois Joseph, age 22, joiner
Balschwiller/ditto   New York

9:0355   22 May 1847
FRELIN, Francois, son of Maurice, age 34, day laborer
Lepuix/--   New York

9:0358   25 May 1847
RAUSS? [PRAUSS?], Jean Michel, age 65, farmer; with
    wife
Haiderbach, Wuerttemberg/Ste.-Marie-aux-Mines
                       New Orleans

9:0360   25 May 1847
RIEHL, Daniel, age 36, farmer
Strasburg/Colmar   New York

9:0368   28 May 1847
WILL? [WITT?], Gregoire, age 38, farmer; with wife &
    4 children
--/Seppois-le-Bas   New York

9:0370   29 May 1847
CHEVENOT, Jacques, age 55, farmer; with son-in-law,
    daughter, grandchild, & maid
--/ Montreux-jeune?   New York

9:0372   29 May 1847
BESANCON, Antoine, age 71, --
Strasbourg/Morvillars   New York

9:0382   02 Jun 1847
CUINEL?, Auguste, age 19, cooper
--/Danjoutin   New York

9:0393   07 Jun 1847
LAUBSER, Joseph, age 34, sawyer
Schlestadt/Guebwiller   New York

9:0394   07 Jun 1847
KAUFFMANN, Catherine, age 24, cook
Massevaux/ditto   New York

9:0398   07 Jun 1847
HUOT, Alexis, age 16, day laborer
--/Evette   New York

9:0402   08 Jun 1847
HOFFMEYER, Joseph, age 43, farmer; with wife & 4
    children
Rouffach/ditto   Jefferson, U.S.A.

9:0403   09 Jun 1847
BURTECHERT, Pierre, age 23, mason; with wife & child
--/Evette   New York

9:0410   14 Jun 1847
KAEMMERLEN, Jean Baptiste, age 19, confectioner
--/St.-Amarin   Augusta, U.S.A.

9:0412   15 Jun 1847
DUBS, Charles, age 21, baker
Ste.-Marie-aux-Mines/ditto   New York

9:0413   15 Jun 1847
ALTHEIMER, Joseph Martin, age 32, brewer?
Thann/Giromagny   ST. Louis, America

9:0425   17 Jun 1847
MEYLING, Joseph, age 30, --?
Soultz/ditto   New York

9:0426   19 Jun 1847
HANAUER, Sebastian, age 33, vine grower; with wife &
    1? child
Soultzmatt/ditto   New York

9:0433   23 Jun 1847
REBISCHEN, Elisabeth, age 48, --; with 2 children
Mulhausen/ditto   Providence, America

9:0436   25 Jun 1847
PEROT, Francois Xavier, age 24, farmer; with wife
--/Valdoie   New Orleans

9:0440   25 Jun 1847
ZIEGER, Henri, age 23, --
Niedermuespach/ditto   Detroit? America

9:0441   26 Jun 1847
HUOT, Jean Baptiste, age 50, --
--/Evette   New York

9:0442   26 Jun 1847
MANGOLD, Antoine, age 53, landowner; with wife
Niedermuespach?/ditto   New York

9:0443   26 Jun 1847
SCHMITT, Antoine, age 25, farmer; with wife & mother-
    in-law
Niedermuespach?/ditto   New York

9:0444   28 Jun 1847
KOEPPLER, Louis, age 29, tinsmith
Colmar/Mulhausen   New York

9:0445   29 Jun 1847
BRENNER?, Louis, age 26, factory worker
Illzach/ditto   New York

9:0452   30 Jun 1847
DREYER, Jean, age 31, mason
Aspach/ditto   New York

9:0455   01 Jul 1847
SCHAVANNE, Ignace, age 22, stonecutter
Aspach/ditto   New York

9:0464   07 Jul 1847
CRENDLE, Edouard, age 20, tinsmith
Mulhouse/ditto   New York

9:0466   07 Jul 1847
DIETRICH, Adolphe, age 22, tinsmith
Turckheim/ditto   New York

9:0467   09 Jul 1847
FAIVRE, Sophie Marie, age 27, dressmaker
Valdieu/ditto   New Orleans

9:0468   09 Jul 1847
FAIVRE, Marie Anne, age 26, dressmaker
Valdieu/ditto   New Orleans

9:0470   10 Jul 1847
RAPINE, Henri Joseph, age 27, joiner; with mother
Willarslesee? [Willars-le-See?]/Lebetain? [Sebetain?]
                                   New York

9:0471   10 Jul 1847
RAPINE, Marie Madeleine, age 17, dressmaker
Willarslesee? [Willars-le-See?]   New York

9:0473   10 Jul 1847
KORB, Charles Xavier, age 21, baker
Thann/ditto   New Orleans

9:0479   12 Jul 1847
MAUSER, Augustin Valentin, age 39, ecclesiastic
Niederhergheim/ditto   New York

9:0483   13 Jul 1847
EGLIN, Felix, age 33, farmer
Argiesans?/ditto   New York

9:0484   13 Jul 1847
HUTZ? [STUTZ?], Jacques, age 44, person of property
Beblinheim/ditto   U.S.A.

9:0485   13 Jul 1847
MONNIN? [MERNNIN?], Francois, age 40, farmer
Argiesaux?/ditto   New York

9:0490   15 Jul 1847
MEYER, Helene, age 24, --
Altkirch/ditto   Thibaudeauville, America

9:0492   16 Jul 1847
DREYFUS, Lehmann, age 40, baker; with wife & 4 chil-
    dren
Rixheim/Mulhouse   New York

9:0495   19 Jul 1847
LAPP, Michel, age 42, --?; with wife & 9? children
Strasbourg/Mulhausen   Providence, America

9:0496   20 Jul 1847
WILD, Georges, age 50, blacksmith; with 4 children
Bartenheim/ditto   New York

9:0499   20 Jul 1847
MOHR, Therese, age 26, --
Brunstatt/ditto   New York

9:0501   20 Jul 1847
DAMOTTE, Francois Georges, age 20, servant
Argiesaux/Bavilliers   New York

9:0502   21 Jul 1847
WEINZAEPFLEN, Michel, age 27, farmer
Ungersheim/ditto   Evanswille [Evansville], America

9:0509   23 Jul 1847
HEROLD, Barbe, age 23, dressmaker
Kaysersberg/ditto   New Orleans

9:0510   23 Jul 1847
EBERHART, Louis, age 26, butcher
Kaysersberg/ditto   New Orleans

9:0514   26 Jul 1847
MOUGEOT, Louis Francois, age 18, brewer
Ste.-Marie-aux-Mines/ditto   New Orleans

9:0517   26 Jul 1847
ROCHLY?, Meinrad, age 40, --; with wife & e children
Hirtzbach/ditto   New York

9:0520   26 Jul 1847
COUTLIERE?, Charles Leroy, age 19, day laborer
Latran?/Valdieux   Detroit, Michigan

9:0524   27 Jul 1847
ERNST, Catherine, nee ZIMMERMANN, age 28, --; with
    sister & 3 children
Thann/ditto   New York

9:0525   27 Jul 1847
ZIMMERMANN, Michel, age 31, sawyer
Hericourt/Thann   New York

9:0527   29 Jul 1847
SCHERTZ, Charles, age 31, joiner; with wife & 1 child
Riediesheim/ditto   New Orleans

9:0537   31 Jul 1847
HARTMANN, Francois Joseph, age 27, mason
Carspach/ditto   New York

9:0538   02 Aug 1847
REFFE?, Jean Georges, age 24, seminarist
Kientzheim/ditto   Dubuque, America

9:0539   02 Aug 1847
SCHIRMER, Marie Anne, age 26, maid
Soultzmatt/Thann   New York

9:0542   02 Aug 1847
SCHULLER, Francois Joseph, age 35, weaver; with wife
    & 2 children
--/Burnhaupt-le-Haut   New York

9:0547   05 Aug 1847
SCHNEIDER, Jean Baptiste, age 20, woodcarver
Husseren (--?)/ditto   Philadelphia

9:0548   05 Aug 1847
HERRMANN, Jean, age 39, --
Mulhouse/ditto   Providence, America

9:0551   07 Aug 1847
DELAYE, Joseph Alexander, age 19, --
Frahier, Haute-Saone/Bavilliers   New Orleans

9:0554   10 Aug 1847
AUGUSTIN, Ignace, age 50, joiner; with wife, 6 chil-
    dren, & his --?
Cernay/Mulhouse   St. Louis, America

9:0562   13 Aug 1847
BONNET?, Francois, age 23, --; with sister
Bessoncourt/ditto   New York

9:0563   13 Aug 1847
FRANCOIS, Jacques, age 26, farmer
Bessoncourt/ditto   New York

9:0568   14 Aug 1847
PETHER, Joseph, age 35, day laborer
Floremont/ditto   New York

9:0573   16 Aug 1847
PFISTER, Ignace, age 30, weaver?
Ostheim/ditto   New York

9:0575   16 Aug 1847
KRUGLEN, Nicholas?, age 33, mason; with wife & chil-
    dren
--/Schweighausen   Columbus, America

9:0576   16 Aug 1847
GSTATTER, Nicholas?, age 23, tailor
--/Schweighausen   Columbus, America

9:0577   16 Aug 1847
HOFFSCHIRR, Madeleine, widow of -- HAGER, age 40,
    tailor
--/Schweigheim   Columbus, America

9:0580   17 Aug 1847
ANDRE, Jean Joseph, age 25, laborer
Liepvre/ditto   New York

9:0581   17 Aug 1847
STANISIERES, Jean-Joseph, age 25, laborer
Liepvre/ditto   New York

9:0582   18 Aug 1847
ZIMBIEHL?, Georges, age 27, woodcarver
Rixheim/ditto   New York

9:0587   20 Aug 1847
RISCH, Chretien, age 36, farmer; with 2 children
Obermichelbach/Hegenheim   New York

9:0588   20 Aug 1847
JACQUOT, Jean Pierre, age 44, baker; with wife & 1
    child
--/Perouse   Detroit, Michigan

34

9:0589   20 Aug 1847
GRAVIER, Jean Baptiste, age 52, landowner; with wife
   & 5 children
--/Perouse   Detroit, Michigan

9:0590   20 Aug 1847
GUIDAT, Jean Baptiste, age 23, joiner
Ste.-Marie-aux-Mines/ditto   New Orleans

9:0591   20 Aug 1847
GERST, Jacques, age 36, spinner; with wife & 2 chil-
   dren
Lehteithal, Bas-Rhin/Mulhouse   New Orlean

9:0592   20 Aug 1847
JODER, Gregoire, age 19, joiner
Mortzwiller/ditto   New York

9:0593   21 Aug 1847
WEBER, Pierre, age 31, factory worker
Bourgfelden/Mulhouse   La Providence, America
                                [Providence, RI?]

9:0594   21 Aug 1847
GERARD, Joseph, age 20, tailor
l'Allemand Rombach [Germany?]/Liepvre   New York

9:0595   21 Aug 1847
HEFTRE?, Marguerite, age 21, worker
Liepvre/ditto   New York

9:0596   21 Aug 1847
MARCHAL, Jean Baptiste, age 19, laborer
Liepvre/ditto   New York

9:0597   21 Aug 1847
ARNOULD, Guirin, age 19, laborer
Liepvre/ditto   New York

9:0598   21 Aug 1847
DAUL, Francois Antoine, age 32, cotton printer
Reschwoog, Bas-Rhin/Mulhouse   La Providence, America
                                [Providence, RI?]

9:0599   21 Aug 1847
DORMOIS, Pierre, age 29, woodcarver
Mulhouse/ditto   La Providence, America
                                [Providence, RI?]

9:0601   23 Aug 1847
HERBST, Andre, age 35, farmer; with wife & 1 child
Guewenheim/ditto   New York

9:0602   23 Aug 1847
GERST, Frederic, age 28, sawyer; with wife & 3 chil-
   dren
Schleithal/Thann   New Orleans

9:0603   23 Aug 1847
GRILLE, Francois, age 29, --; with wife & 1 child
Belfort/ditto   New Orleans

9:0604   23 Aug 1847
BECK, Francois Antoine, age 49, farmer; with wife &
   5 children
Sentheim/Lauw   Ohio

9:0606   23 Aug 1847
PARIS, Pierre, age 39, weaver; with wife & 3 children
Echenaus?, Haute-Saone/Mulhouse   New Orleans

9:0608   24 Aug 1847
SEGUIN, David?, age 21, metal turner
Mulhouse/ditto   St. Louis, America

9:0609   25 Aug 1847
HEINRICH, Abraham, age 29, farmer?
Illzach/ditto   Boston, America

9:0610   28 Aug 1847
BACKEL, Jean, age 51, day laborer; with wife & 7
   children
Guemar/ditto   New York

9:0611   26 Aug 1847
MORTEAU, Marianne, age 26, dressmaker; with son
Danjoutin/ditto   New Orleans

9:0612   26 Aug 1847
BIEHLMANN, Antoine, age 57, joiner; with wife, 2
   daughters? & 1 grandson?
Guewenheim/ditto   Ohio

9:0613   27 Aug 1847
SCHNEBELEN, Meinrad, age 30, joiner
Sentheim/ditto   New York

9:0614   27 Aug 1847
ROTH, Dagobert, age 29, farmer; with wife, sister, &
   7 children
Sentheim/ditto   New York

9:0615   27 Aug 1847
RIGLY, Pierre, age 24, day laborer
Illhaeusern/ditto   Bitzbourg [Pittsburgh?] America

9:0616   27 Aug 1847
DROZ, Maximin, age 47, day laborer; with wife, --?, &
   6 children
Illhaeusern/ditto   Bitzbourg [Pittsburgh?] America

9:0618   30 Aug 1847
SUTTER? [FUTTER?], Thiebaud, age 31, farmer
--/Sentheim   New York

9:0625   01 Sep 1847
GEBEL, Joseph, age 18, tailor
Massevaux [Masevaux]/ditto   St. Louis, America

9:0627   01 Sep 1847
TURIN? [CURIN?], Aloys, age 30, tinsmith
Massevaux [Masevaux]/ditto   St. Louis, America

9:0631   02 Sep 1847
COLLIGNON, Joseph, age 33, wheelwright
Liepvre/ditto   New Orleans

9:0632   02 Sep 1847
HUVIE?, Marie Francoise, age 24
Liepvre/ditto   New Orleans

9:0633   02 Sep 1847
BIHL, Gaspard, age 40, laborer; with wife & 5 chil-
    dren
Brechaumont/ditto   New York

9:0635   02 Sep 1847
MINNIES?, Jean Dominque, age 20, factory worker
Liepvre/ditto   New Orleans

9:0636   02 Sep 1847
COLLIN, Henry, age 20, saddler
Liepvre/ditto   New Orleans

9:0637   02 Sep 1847
MULLER, Jean Baptiste, age 36, --?; with wife & 2
    children
Liepvre/ditto   New Orleans

9:0638   02 Sep 1847
BOLLE, Joseph, age 29, farmer; with wife & 1 child
Liepvre/ditto   New Orleans

9:0639   02 Sep 1847
HENRY, Jean Baptiste, age 30, farmer
Liepvre/ditto   New Orleans

9:0642   03 Sep 1847
GROSJEAN, Pierre Paul, age 31, designer; with wife &
    2 children
Rorsch--? [Rohrschwihr? Rorschach?]/Mulhausen
                            Providence, America

9:0643   03 Sep 1847
SOEHNLE, Joseph, age 48, butcher?; with wife & 2
    children
Burbach?-le-Bas/Lauw   Ohio

9:0645   04 Sep 1847
KRETZ, Auguste, age 26, businessman
Bliescastel?, Rhenish Bavaria/Mulhausen   New York

9:0646   04 Sep 1847
PRENAT, Pierre Fidel, age 43, tailer; with wife & 8?
    children
Villars-le-BAs/ditto   New York

9:0648   04 Sep 1847
KIEFFER, Joseph, age 33, day laborer
Roderen?/ditto   Baltimore

9:0649   04 Sep 1847
PRENAT, Jean Baptiste Constant?, age 19, day laborer
Villars-le-Bas/ditto   New York

9:0650   06 Sep 1847
GREDER? [GRECLER?], Louis, age 22, carpenter
Hegenheim/ditto   New York

9:0651   06 Sep 1847
RITSCH, Francois, age 28?, carpenter; with brother
Thann/ditto   New York

9:0652   06 Sep 1847
GRIMAUD?, Nicolas, age 67, handworker; with wife & 3
    children
Eteimbes/Cernay   New York

9:0657   07 Sep 1847
NAGEOTTE, Louis, age 16, tailor
Vaujaumont?, Doubs/Villars-le-Bas?   New York

9:0659   07 Sep 1847
ANCKLIN, Laurent Paul, age 25, servant
Liesberg, Switzerland/Kientzheim   New York

9:0660   07 Sep 1847
EHRHART, Barbe, age 18, servant
Thann/ditto   Philadelphia

9:0663   09 Sep 1847
WALTZER, Louis, age 27, farmer
Sentheim/ditto   New York

9:0667   10 Sep 1847
PY, Jean Pierre, age 48, farmer; with wife & 6? chil-
    dren
Eguenique/ditto   Philadelphia

9:0669   13 Sep 1847
EHRET, Catherine, age 23, weaver
Rammersmatt/Bourbach-le-Bas   New York

9:0671   13 Sep 1847
SUTTER, Aloyse, age 25, spinner
Sentheim/ditto   New York

9:0673   13 Sep 1847
PIERRE, Jean Georges, age 19, weaver
Liepvre/ditto   New Orleans

9:0676   14 Sep 1847
HERBSTER, Phillipe, age 24, sawyer
Massevaux/Guebwiller   New York

9:0677   14 Sep 1847
DEUTSCH, Jean Mathias, age 34, cooper & brazier?;
    with wife & 2 children
Birmisheim, Rhenish Prussia/Moosch   New York

9:0678   16 Sep 1847
BERNARD, Francois Xavier, age 25, woodturner
--/Massevaux   St. Louis, America

9:0679   16 Sep 1847
BITSCH, Jean Baptiste, age 21, cloth printer
Pfastatt/ditto   New York

9:0688   16 Sep 1847
FUCHS, Georges, age 22, joiner; with brother
Liepvre/ditto   New Orleans

9:0681   18 Sep 1847
POURCHOT, Jacques Frederic, age 48, mechanical worker
    with wife & 2 children
Beaucourt/ditto   New York

9:0682   20 Sep 1847
VIENOT, Jean, age 42, factory worker; with mother, 2
    sisters, 3 brothers, & his nephew
Roches, Doubs/Mulhouse   New York

9:0683   20 Sep 1847
VIENOT, Pierre, age 32, metal turner
Roches, Doubs/Mulhouse   New York

9:0685   20 Sep 1847
PASSON? [PAYSON?], Francois?, age 49, farmer; with
    wife, 2 children, & father
Angeot/ditto   Jacksonville, America

9:0690   23 Sep 1847
BLANC, Jacques, age 37, factory worker; with mother-
    in-law & 3 children
Liesberg, Switzerland/Sentheim   New York

9:0693   25 Sep 1847
GERSPACHER, Joseph, age 29, --? for mechanical ma-
    chines
Oberherschingen, Baden/Guebwiller   New York

9:0694   25 Sep 1847
ROTHMUND, Marie Anne, age 25, maid
Guebwiller/ditto   Utika [Utica?], America

9:0696   27 Sep 1847
BECHLE, Ferdinand, age 21, carpenter
Cernay/ditto   New York

9:0697   27 Sep 1847
BAUER, Michel, age 52?, wheelwright; with wife, 5
    children, & 1 servant
Beblenheim/Massevaux   San Antonio de Bexar, Texas

9:0698   27 Sep 1847
PERRIN, Etienne, age 46, farmer; with wife & 6 chil-
    dren
La-Bresse, Vosges/Massevaux
                          San Antonio de Bexar, Texas

9:0699   27 Sep 1847
BACHER, Valentin, age 31, tailer
Hegenheim/ditto   New York

9:0700   27 Sep 1847
DESPOIRER? [DESPOIRES?], Jean Baptiste, age 52, far-
    mer; with wife & maid
Evette/ditto   New York

9:0706   30 Sep 1847
PEUGEUT, Antoine, age 59, tailor; with wife & 3 chil-
    dren
Offemont/ditto   New York

9:0710   01 Oct 1847
CHAVANNE, Therese, age 25, dressmaker
--/Massevaux   New York

9:0714   04 Oct 1847
ROY, Nicolas, age 23, farmer
--/Angeot   New York

9:0715   06 Oct 1847
FLUEHR, Protee?, age 40, spinner; with wife & 3 chil-
    dren
Lauw/Bollwiller   New York

9:0716   06 Oct 1847
FLUEHR, Martin, age 52, farmer
--/Bollwiller   New York

9:0719   07 Oct 1847
WETZEL, Jean, age 23, blacksmith
Buellwiller [Bollwiller?]/Mulhouse?   New York

9:0722   07 Oct 1847
ROMOND, Jean Claude Celestin, age 23, farmer
--/Urcerey?   New York

9:0723   07 Oct 1847
GIEDELMANN, Francois Xavier, age 33, cabinetmaker;
    with wife, 1 child, & mother-in-law
Massevaux/ditto   St. Louis, America

9:0725   08 Oct 1847
BLUM, Madeleine, nee PIERCON, age 41; with 3 children
Bretagne/Thann   New York

9:0726   08 Oct 1847
MAURER, Georges, age 16, farmer
--? allemand/Rombach   New Orleans

9:0727   08 Oct 1847
BISSER, David, age 21, factory worker
Guebwiller/Mulhouse   New York

9:0729   09 Oct 1847
IHLER, Charles, age 20, locksmith
Massevaux/ditto   New Orleans

9:0730   09 Oct 1847
FLEIG, Antoine, age 42, blacksmith; with wife,
    father-in-law, & 5? brothers?
Boerach, Bas-Rhin/Massevaux   St. Louis, America

9:0731   11 Oct 1847
VOELCKER? [VAELCKER?], Michel, age 35, machinist
Orschwihr?/Buehl   New York

9:0732   11 Oct 1847
BOUILLARD, Jean Pierre, age 19, saddler
Danjoutin/Belfort   New York

9:0737   12 Oct 1847
OBERLAND, Marie Henry Victor, age 27, clerk --?
Belfort/Colmar   New York

9:0740   12 Oct 1847
FOURG, Jean Joseph, age 24, farmer
l'Allemand?/Rombach   New Orleans

9:0741   13 Oct 1847
ILTIS?, Francoise, age 22, weaver
Lewen?/ditto   Castroville, Texas

9:0743   14 Oct 1847
WELDY, Andre, age 70, farmer; with his child
Oberhergheim/ditto   New York

9:0744   14 Oct 1847
WELDY, Jean, age 36, day laborer; with wife & 4 chil-
    dren
Oberhergheim/ditto   New York

9:0745   14 Oct 1847
WEINGARTHNER, Martin, age 38, day laborer; with wife
    & 4 children
Oberhergheim/ditto   New York

9:0746   14 Oct 1847
QUICKERT, Conrad, age 44, weaver; with wife & 3 chil-
    dren
Oberhergheim./ditto   New York

9:0747   14 Oct 1847
QUICKERT, Xavier, age 35, day laborer; with wife & 2
    children
Oberhergheim/ditto   New York

9:0757   19 Oct 1847
CHEVIRON, Eugene, age 21?, weigher
Bar-le-Duc? [Bas-le-Duc?]/Cernay   New York

9:0760   20 Oct 1847
PFAFF, Nicolas, age 51, day laborer; with wife,
    mother, & 5 children
Kembs/Rixheim   New Orleans

9:0761   21 Oct 1847
QUICKERT, Leger, age 37, mason
Oberhergheim/ditto   New York

9:0762   21 Oct 1847
QUICKERT, Antoine, age 31, mason
Oberhergheim/ditto   New York

9:0763   21 Oct 1847
LEISY, Jean, age 27, businessman
Colmar/Mulhausen   New Orleans

9:0764   21 Oct 1847
MEINSOHN, Jean Baptiste, age 25, farmer
--/Cernay   New Orleans

9:0766   22 Oct 1847
L'HOTE, Ambroise, age 22, cooper
Urcerey/Valdoie   New York

8:0768   22 Oct 1847
FUCHS, Georges, age 45, mason
Ihringen, Baden/Mulhouse   New York

9:0771   23 Oct 1847
VAEGELY, Fidele, age 25, cabinetmaker; with wife, son
    & brother
Cernay/ditto   New Orleans

9:0773   25 Oct 1847
MULLER, Joseph, age 22, tailor
--/Oberhagenthal   Cincinnati

9:0780   28 Oct 1847
MUSSLIN, Sebastien, age 47, day laborer; with wife &
    6 children
Rixheim/ditto   Castroville, Texas

9:0781   28 Oct 1847
WAGNER, Seraphin, age 23, farmer; with wife & child
Rixheim/ditto   Castroville, Texas

9:0786   29 Oct 1847
WUERLENSCHLAG, Jacques, age 24?, gleaner?
Cernay/Soppe-le-Bas   New York

9:0789   02 Nov 1847
WALTER? [WALLER?], Frederic, age 34, cabinetmaker;
    with wife & son
Mulhausen/ditto   New Orleans

9:0791   02 Nov 1847
MURINGER, Thiebaud, age 47, day laborer; with wife,
    sister, & 5 children
Steinbach/ditto   New York

9:0792   02 Nov 1847
MARCK, Antoine, age 49, coachman?
Luatenbach --?/Ensisheim   Texas

9:0794   03 Oct 1847
RIOTTE, Jean Pierre, age 37, farmer; with wife & 4
    children
Ste.-Croix-aux-Mines/ditto   New Orleans

9:0795   03 Nov 1847
PAIRIR, Nicolas, age 27, weaver
Ste.-Croix-aux-Mines/ditto   New Orleans

9:0800   06 Nov 1847
HOFER, Marie Elisabeth, wife of -- KUNG, age 29, with
    1 child
Niederwyl, Switzerland/Mulhouse   New York

9:0804   10 Nov 1847
HEITZ, Jean Baptiste, age 25, farmer
Kembs/ditto   New York

9:0805   13 Nov 1847
FALCINELLA, Elisabeth, age 40, dressmaker
Kaysersberg/Colmar   New York

9:0806   13 Nov 1847
VONAU, Ignace, age 47, blacksmith
Schwobweiller, Bas-Rhin/Cernay   Victoria, Texas

9:0807   15 Nov 1847
TOEKLER, Xavier, age 38, joiner; with 2 sisters-in-
    law
Offemont/ditto   Victoria, Texas

9:0811   17 Nov 1847
CRITZ, Joseph, age 52, landowner; with wife, 7 chil-
    dren, & 2 maids
Guewenatten/Angeot   Columbus, America

9:0815   19 Nov 1847
WINTER, Godefroy Ernest, age 26, tannery worker
Backnang, Wuerttemberg/Vieux-Thann   New York

9:0816   19 Nov 1847
RIEGGER, Jean Nepomucene, age 22, carpenter
Zepfenhorn, Wuerttemberg/Vieux-Thann   New York

9:0818   19 Nov 1847
LUDWIG, Catherine, age --, --; with 4 children
Herrlisheim/ditto   New Orleans

9:0824   27 Nov 1847
ROTH, Henry, age 39, weaver; with wife & 3 children
Bourbach-le-Bas/ditto   New York

9:0825   27 Nov 1847
MEYER, Joseph, age 59, day laborer; with wife & 4
    children
Bourbach-le-Bas/ditto   New York

9:0829   27 Nov 1847
RICH, Marie Anne, age 33?, housekeeper; with brothers
Orschwihr? [Orschwiller?]/ditto   Castroville, Texas

9:0830   29 Nov 1847
GRETZINGER, Ignace, age 28, cooper
--/Runnersheim?   New York

9:0833   01 Dec 1847
BISSLER, Jean, age 57, farmer; with 2 children
Bourbach-le-Bas/ditto   New York

9:0834   01 Dec 1847
BISSLER, Ferdinand, age 24, day laborer; with wife
Bourbach-le-Bas/ditto   New York

9:0835   01 Dec 1847
DISTOR?, Jean, age 26, metal turner; with wife
Hupach (sur de Massevaux)/Bourbach-le-Bas   New York

9:0837   01 Dec 1847
FUERLING, Philippe, age 34, tailor
Roggenhouse/ditto   New York

9:0838   01 Dec 1847
STRUSSER, Laurent, age 20, servant
Hirtzfelden/ditto   New York

9:0839   01 Dec 1847
HABERBUSCH, Jean, age 50, shoemaker; with wife, 8?
    children, & brother-in-law
Rumersheim/Hirtzfelden   New York

9:0840   01 Dec 1847
SCHMITT, Antoine, age 27, farmer; with wife, children,
    & natural brother
Hirtzfelden/ditto   New York

9:0841   02 Dec 1847
HAFFNER, Sebastien, age 17, shoemaker
Bourbach-le-Bas/Guewenatten   New York

9:0842   02 Dec 1847
SCHERRER, Joseph, age 34, shoemaker; with wife & 5
    children
Traubach-le-Haut/Guewenatten   New York

9:0844   03 Dec 1847
SCHERRER, Jean, age 26, carpenter
Riechen, Switzerland/Mulhouse   New York

9:0847   04 Dec 1847
KNECHT, Josephine, age 23, office girl
Sentheim/ditto   New York

9:0850   06 Dec 1847
RISS, Ignace, age 27, salesman
Sentheim/ditto   New York

9:0851   06 Dec 1847
REISSER, Joseph, age 20, tailor
Guebwiller/ditto   New York

9:0854   09 Dec 1847
BLONDE, Joseph, age 62, laborer; with wife, 3 chil-
dren, & brother
Traubach-le-Haut/ditto   New York

9:0857   11 Dec 1847
HAUPTMANN, Joseph, age 28, joiner
Soultzmatt/ditto   New Orleans

9:0858   11 Dec 1847
HEITZMANN, Xavier, age 28, laborer
Soultzmatt/ditto   New Orleans

9:0859   11 Dec 1847
KNUEPFFLE, Jean, age 50, shoemaker; with his son
Colmar/ditto   New Orleans

9:0866   16 Dec 1847
SCHERRER, Paul, age 39, weaver; with wife & 3 chil-
dren
Traubach-le-Haut/ditto   New York

9:0869   17 Dec 1847
HUESSER, Joseph, age 57, farmer; with 4 children
Wittelsheim/ditto   New York

9:0873   23 Dec 1847
STAHL, Francois Xavier, age 37, vintner
Orschwihr/ditto   Castroville, Texas

9:0874   23 Dec 1847
PFEIFFER, Gaspard, age 48, day laborer; with wife & 3
children
Langenschleitel, Bas-Rhin/Bladelsheim?   New York

9:0879   29 Dec 1847
BURGUNDER, Seraphin, age 32, joiner; with wife &
nephew
--/Ranspach   New York

9:0881   30 Dec 1847
ERCK, Jean Antoine, age 49, baker; with wife & 3
children
Herrlisheim/ditto   St. Louis, America

9:0882   30 Dec 1847
KUEN, Jean, age 37, shoemaker; with wife & 2 children
Herrlisheim/ditto   St. Louis, America

BIRY, 8:2513, 8:3118

BIRY. See also BURY

BISSER, 9:0727

BISSLER, 9:0833, 9:0834

BITSCH, 8:2860, 8:2939, 9:0076, 9:0679

BITSCH. See also BOETSCH

BITTERLIN, 8:3131

BLANC, 9:0690

BLANC. See also WEISS (translation)

BLASIARD, 8:2003

BLEYER, 8:1736, 8:1752, 8:3006, 8:3007

BLISS, 8:2688

BLONDE, 8:2550, 9:0054, 9:0055, 9:0854

BLUM, 9:0725

BLUSS, 8:2098

BOBENRIETH, 8:1692, 8:1963, 8:2957

BOEGLIN, 8:2230

BOETSCH, 8:1885, 8:1947

BOETSCH. See also BITSCH

BOGEN, 8:3473

BOHL, 9:0157

BOIGY, 8:2231

BOLLE, 9:0638

BOLZY, 8:2463

BONAT, 8:2629

BONNET, 9:0562

BOSSLER, 8:2369

BOTZY, 8:2463

BOUCHEZ, 8:3475, 8:3478, 9:0257

BOUILLARD, 9:0732

BOURGUARD, 8:3064

BOURGUIN, 8:3125

BOURGUNIOT, 8:2063

BRAND, 8:2457

BRANDSTETTER. See BANDSTETTER

BRAUN, 9:0339

BRECHBUHLER, 8:1817

BRENNER, 9:0445

BRENNER. See also BRONNER, BRUNNER

BRIDEN, 8:3108

BRONNER, 9:0048

BRONNER. See also BRENNER, BRUNNER

BROYEZ, 8:3464

BRUCK, 8:3079

BRUNNER, 9:0121

BRUNNER. See also BRENNER, BRONNER

BUBSER, 8:3425

BUCHER, 9:0269

BUEHER, 9:0269

BUERRER, 8:2207

BUERRER. See also BARRER, BIRRER, BURRER

BURGER, 8:3323

BURGER. See also BERGER

BURGUNDER, 9:0879

BURGY, 8:3261

BURLEN, 8:2680

BURLIAT, 8:1728, 8:1750

BURNER, 9:0080

BURRER, 8:2217, 8:2525, 8:2889, 8:2945

BURRER. See also BARRER, BIRRER, BUERRER

BURTECHERT, 9:0403

BURY, 8:1763

BURY. See also BIRY

BUSSLER, 8:2803

CACHOT, 8:2406

CAYOT, 8:2625, 8:2633, 8:3190

CHABOUDE, 8:1836

CHANEY, 8:2569

CHAPPE, 8:2135

CHAPUIS, 8:1742, 8:1756, 8:3196, 8:3197, 8:3444

CHARPIAT, 8:1967

CHARTON, 8:2669

CHATELOT, 8:2577

CHATILLON, 8:2533

CHAVANNE, 9:0183, 9:0710

CHAVANNE. See also SCHAVANNE

CHERAY, 8:3049

CHEVENOT, 9:0370

CHEVIRON, 9:0757

CHRISTEN, 8:1688, 9:0210, 9:0349

CLER, 8:1805, 9:0057

CLOR, 8:1727, 9:0191

CLOR. See also KLUR

CLORS, 9:0191

COCK, 9:0133

COHEN. See KUEN

COLLIGNON, 9:0631

COLLIN, 9:0636

COUNNERY, 8:1814

COURTOT, 8:3290, 8:3293

COUSIN. See VETTER (translation)

COUTLIERE, 9:0520

COUVET, 8:3412

CRANELTER, 8:3110

CRAVE, 8:3455

CRENDLE, 9:0464

CRIGLER, 8:3148

CRITZ, 8:1812, 9:0811

CRITZ. See also KRETZ

CUINEL, 9:0382

CUISINIER, 8:3405

CURIN, 9:0627

CUYOT, 8:2625, 8:2633, 8:3335

DAEGELEN, 8:2842

DAMOTTE, 9:0501

DANCOURT, 8:1860

DANEOURT, 8:1860

DANHEISER, 8:2791

DANHEISES, 8:2791

DANIEL, 8:1769

DATTLER, 9:0013

DAUL, 9:0598

DECKERT, 8:3271

DEGENHARD, 8:2527, 8:2528

DEIBER, 8:3013

DEIBES, 8:3013

DELACROIX, 8:3447

DELAET, 8:3466, 9:0019

DELAYE, 9:0551

DELIMSCH, 9:0022

DELLUNG, 9:0240

DESDAMES, 8:2624, 8:2987

DESPOIRER, 9:0700

DESPOIRES, 9:0700

DEUR, 8:3383, 9:0190

DEUS, 9:0190

DEUTSCH, 9:0677

DEUX, 8:3383

DIDIER, 8:1824

DIESTELRATH, 8:2706

DIETAMANN, 8:1863

DIETEMANN, 8:2837

DIETERLE, 8:2171

DIETRICH, 8:2166,
9:0067, 9:0466

DISTOR, 9:0835

DOLLFUS, 8:2108

DONZE, 9:0053

DOPPLER, 8:3087

DORMOIS, 8:2571, 9:0599

DREY, 8:1783, 8:2481

DREYER, 8:2035, 9:0452

DREYFUS, 9:0492

DROZ, 8:2554, 8:2774,
8:3380, 9:0616

DRUY, 8:1783

DUBORONSKI, 9:0003

DUBS, 9:0412

DUCLOUX, 8:2641

DUPRE, 8:2676, 9:0027

DUPREZ, 9:0138, 9:0139

DURACHER, 8:3435

DURLIOT, 9:0059

DUVIE, 8:2775

EBERHART, 9:0510

EGLE, 9:0029

EGLIN, 9:0483

EHLINGER, 8:2146,
8:2745, 8:2746, 9:0017

EHRET, 8:2368, 8:2386,
9:0097, 9:0208,
9:0265, 9:0669

EHRHART, 9:0660

EHRHART. See also
ERHART

EICHER, 9:0222

EICHES, 8:1864

EICHINGER, 8:1740

ENDERLEN, 8:3167,
8:3393, 9:0236

ENGELHART, 8:2243

ERCK, 9:0881

ERHARD, 8:2734, 8:2831

ERHART. See also
EHRHART

ERNST, 8:3189, 9:0524

ESCHEMANN, 8:3040

EUHER, 8:1864

FAHRNER, 8:2397, 8:2398,
8:2399, 8:3356

FAIVRE, 8:2646, 8:2648,
9:0467, 9:0468

FALCINELLA, 9:0805

FAURE, 8:2183

FEBER, 9:0298, 9:0326

FELLMANN, 9:0123

FERAND, 9:0039

FERARD, 9:0039

FEST, 8:3146

FEUTE, 9:0115

FIAT, 9:0158

FINCK, 8:2449

FINGER, 8:3085

FINSTERBACH, 9:0115

FISCHER, 8:2643, 8:3485,
9:0035, 9:0308

FLEIG, 9:0730

FLEURY, 8:2640, 9:0005,
9:0323

FLIDLER, 8:1709

FLIELLER, 8:1709

FLOTAT, 8:3427

FLUEHR, 9:0715, 9:0716

FOLLMANN, 9:0123

FOLLOT, 8:2824

FOLTZ, 9:0255

FORSTER, 8:3484

FORWENDEL, 8:3203

FOURG, 9:0740

FOURNIER, 8:2632

FRANCOIS, 9:0563

FRECHARD, 8:2771

FRELIN, 9:0355

FREUDENREICH, 8:1923

FREY, 8:1762, 8:1990,
9:0149

FREYBARGER, 8:2556

FREYBOURGER, 8:1765,
8:1853, 8:1897, 8:3194

FREYBURGER, 8:2556,
8:3260

FREYENBERGER, 8:2605

FRICK, 9:0110

FRICKER, 8:3075

FROEHLY, 9:0172, 9:0174

FROELICH, 9:0217

FROMALD, 8:2156

FUCHS, 8:2165, 8:3122,
8:3422, 9:0688, 9:0768

FUERLING, 9:0837

FUERSTENBERGER, 8:3104

FUHRNER, 8:2397, 8:2398,
8:2399

FUNK, 8:2085

FURLINDER, 9:0098

FUTTER, 9:0618

GABLER, 8:3139

GAECHTER, 8:3089

GALLIET, 8:1835

GANGLER, 8:3194

GARTEISEN, 8:3082

GASPERMENT, 8:2420

GASSER, 8:1773

GASSET, 9:0016

GAST, 8:3448

GEBEL, 9:0625

GEIL, 8:1808

GEISS, 8:1962

GERARD, 8:3054, 9:0594

GERSPACHER, 9:0693

GERST, 9:0591, 9:0602

GERTHOFER, 8:2808

GERTHOFFER, 8:2809,
9:0211, 9:0243

GERTHOFFES, 8:2809

GETSCHY, 9:0266

GEYMANN, 8:1909

GIEDELMANN, 9:0723

GINOT, 9:0179

GIRARDEY, 8:2070

GIRARDHEY, 8:2998

GIRARDOT, 8:1957

GIRLOT, 8:3390

GISSINGER, 8:2390,
8:3368

GISSINGES, 8:2390

GLADIEUX, 8:1754

GOEPFERT, 8:1930

GOETZ, 9:0264

GOMMENGINGER, 9:0244

GOUSSET, 8:3254

GOUTTERMANN, 9:0113

GRAF, 9:0065

GRAVIER, 9:0589

GRAWEY, 8:2678

GRAWEY. See also GREI-
VEY

GRECLER, 9:0650

GREDER, 9:0650

GREIVEY, 8:1876

GREIVEY. See also GRA-
WEY

GRENAH, 8:3115

GRENAT, 8:3115

GRETZINGER, 9:0830

GREWEY, 8:1876

GREWEY. See also GRA-
WEY

GRIESEMANN, 8:1837

GRILLE, 9:0603

GRILLOT, 8:3168

GRIMAUD, 9:0652

GRISEZ, 8:1741, 9:0040, 9:0041

GROB, 8:1780

GROS, 8:2858

GROSHAENY, 8:2584

GROSJEAN, 8:2603, 8:3426, 9:0207, 9:0642

GROSS, 8:1718, 8:1780

GRUBER, 8:3223

GRUNINGER, 8:3041

GRUSSI, 8:3308

GSCHWIND, 8:2005, 9:0014

GSTATTER, 9:0576

GUERRINGE, 9:0083

GUIDAT, 9:0590

GUILLARD, 8:3428

GUILLAUME, 8:2023, 8:2025

GUILLAUMEY, 8:3336

GUILLINGER, 8:2628

GUITTARD, 8:3428, 8:3441

GULLY, 8:1846, 8:1899

GUNDY, 8:3366, 8:3367

GURMELY, 8:2400

GUTHMANN, 9:0178

GUTZWILLER, 9:0147, 9:0171

HAAS, 8:2874

HABERBUSCH, 9:0839

HABERSTOCK, 8:3482

HABERSTROH, 8:2061

HABERTHUR, 8:2709

HABETROH, 8:2061

HABY, 8:3111

HADIEUX, 8:1754

HAFFNER, 9:0841

HAGEMUELLER, 8:3137

HAGENMULLER, 8:3137

HAGER, 8:2708, 8:2733, 9:0577

HALDY, 8:2996

HALLER, 8:2130

HAMALLE, 8:3151

HANAUER, 9:0074, 9:0426

HANS, 8:1689, 9:0205

HANSBERGER, 8:2361

HANTZ, 8:2169, 8:2170, 8:2913

HARTMANN, 8:3155, 8:3253, 9:0537

HASSENFRATZ, 8:3376

HATIE, 8:2524

HAUCK, 8:2162

HAUPTMANN, 9:0857

HAUS, 8:1689

HECK, 8:1768, 9:0135

HECKLY, 8:2855

HEFTRE, 9:0595

HEIBERGER, 8:3025

HEIM, 9:0214

HEIMBRECHT, 8:3129

HEINMELIN, 9:0324

HEINRICH, 9:0609

HEINRICH. See also HENRY (translation)

HEINZ, 9:0069

HEISLEN, 8:2447

HEITZ, 9:0804

HEITZEMANN, 8:1966

HEITZMANN, 9:0858

HELD, 8:1816

HELLER, 9:0202

HEMELEN, 8:3407

HEMMELIN, 9:0324

HEMMERLE, 8:1811

HENCKY, 9:0167

HENNY, 8:2515

HENRY, 9:0639

HENRY. See also HEINRICH (translation)

HENZEL, 8:1696

HERBST, 9:0601

HERBSTER, 9:0676

HERMANN, 8:3127

HEROLD, 9:0509

HERRMANN, 9:0548

HERSCHBERGER, 9:0209

HESS, 8:3467

HESTIN, 8:3238

HETTERLIN, 8:2492

HEYER, 9:0023

HEYLANDT, 8:3096, 8:3187

HINDERMANN, 9:0219

HINGUE, 8:3449

HINTZY, 9:0306

HIROT, 9:0226

HIRTZLIN, 8:2352

HOEFFIGER, 8:1851

HOFER, 9:0800

HOFFERT, 8:3388

HOFFMEYER, 9:0402

HOFFSCHIRR, 9:0577

HORNER, 9:0239

HORNES, 9:0239

HORNUNG, 8:2738

HORNY, 8:1896

HOTZ, 8:3294

HUDER, 9:0193

HUESSER, 9:0869

HUFF, 8:3296

HUG, 8:2177, 8:2853, 8:3219

HUGUENOT, 8:3278

HUNSINGER, 8:2645

HUNTER. See JAEGER (translation)

HUOT, 9:0398, 9:0441

HUSSER, 9:0128

HUSUBRECHT, 8:3129

HUTZ, 9:0484

HUTZLER, 8:3066, 8:3076

HUVIE, 9:0632

IHLER, 9:0729

ILTIS, 8:1968, 9:0741

INGOLD, 8:2164

JABLER, 8:3139

JACQUEMIN, 8:2182, 8:2711, 8:2712

JACQUOT, 8:2776, 8:3257, 9:0588

JAEGER, 9;0146

JAEGLIN, 9:0015

JAKOB, 8:1708

JARDON, 8:3475

JARDON. See also JOURDAIN

JECKER, 8:3166

JELIDON, 8:2859

JENN, 8:1780, 8:1875

JETTER, 8:3166

JODER, 8:1799, 8:2941, 9:0592

JOLIER, 9:0136

JOUN, 9:0247

JOURDAIN, 8:3286

JOURDAIN. See also JARDON

JUDLIN, 9:0279

JUEN, 8:2740

KABIS, 9:0218

KAEHLER, 9:0327

KAEHLER. See also
  KOHLER

KAEMMERLIN, 9:0410

KAEPPELIN, 9:0267

KALTENBACH, 8:1937

KASTLER, 8:1838

KAUFFMANN, 8:3107,
  8:3179, 9:0394

KAUFMANN, 8:1684, 8:1714

KAYSER, 8:1951

KELLER, 8:3081, 8:3090,
  9:0081

KEMPF, 8:1906, 8:3073,
  8:3465

KEMPFF, 8:2459

KIBLER, 8:1845

KIEFFER, 8:2180, 9:0648

KIELSCH, 9:0228

KIEMBLER, 8:2069

KIENE, 8:3102, 8:3404,
  8:3408, 9:0077

KIENER, 8:3083

KINNENBERG, 9:0132

KIRCHMEYER, 8:2159

KIRLOT, 8:3390

KIRMENBERGER, 9:0132

KLEIN, 8:3005, 9:0216

KLEPFFENSTEIN, 8:2618

KLINGER, 8:1866

KLOETZLEN, 8:3389

KLOPFENSTEIN, 8:2618,
  8:3410

KLUR, 8:3135

KLUR. See also CLOR

KNAUSS, 8:2674, 8:2685

KNECHT, 9:0847

KNITTEL, 8:2681

KNUEPFFLE, 9:0859

KOEGLER, 8:3363, 8:3432

KOEPPLER, 9:0444

KOHLER, 8:1818

KOHLER. See also
  KAEHLER

KOLB, 8:2365

KOLL, 8:3012

KOOS, 8:2366, 8:2945

KORB, 9:0473

KRAMCK, 8:1795

KRANICK, 8:1795

KRAUSHAAR, 8:3086

KRAUSS, 8:2685

KREKLER. See GREGLER

KRETZ, 9:0645

KRETZ. See also CRITZ

KRUGLEN, 9:0575

KRUST, 8:2432

KUEN, 9:0105, 9:0882

KUENEMANN, 8:2894

KUHN, 8:2871

KULSCH, 9:0228

KUNG, 9:0800

KURZMANN, 8:2956

L'HOMME, 8:3279

L'HOTE, 9:0766

LABOUEBE, 9:0184

LAGEZ, 9:0155

LAHMANN, 8:1851

LAIBE, 9:0166

LAMBOLE, 8:2563

LAPP, 9:0495

LATSCH, 8:2664

LAUBSER, 9:0393

LAVAL, 8:2555

LEIPZIG. See LIBSIG

LEFEVRE, 8:3174

LEGAISSE, 8:3340

LEHMANN. See LAHMANN

LEINS, 8:2241

LEISY, 8:3247, 9:0763

LEMAIRE, 8:2354, 9:0270

LENGELIN, 8:3235

LENHERR, 8:2934

LENTZ, 8:3397

LESTER, 8:2758

LEVEQUE, 8:2963

LIBRE, 8:3234, 9:0028

LIBSIG, 8:2232

LIEBELIN, 8:3195, 8:3252

LIECHLE, 8:1794

LIEFFERMANN, 9:0223

LIEGNIAC, 8:2242

LINCK, 8:1789

LINDER, 9:0200

LINGRUEN, 8:3152

LINZENBOLTZ, 8:2129

LINZENHOLTZ, 8:2129

LINZENMEYER, 8:3141

LIROT, 8:3342, 9:0226

LITIGUE, 8:3221

LITIQUE, 8:2769

LITTLE. See KLEIN
  (translation)

LITZLER, 8:2567

LOEW, 8:3162

LOEWENGUTH, 8:2057

LOILLIER, 9:0199

LOPINOT, 8:1932

LORENTZ, 8:2558

LOUIS, 8:3060, 8:3378

LUDWIG, 9:0818

MADRU, 8:1888, 8:2535

MAETHER, 9:0220

MAGER, 9:0073

MAIGRAT, 8:3406

MAIGROT, 8:3406

MAILLARD, 8:1739, 8:1751

MAITRE, 8:2642, 9:0127

MANGOLD, 9:0442

MANN, 8:3112

MARCHAL, 9:0596

MARCHAND, 8:2153,
  8:2569, 8:2585

MARCK, 9:0792

MARCONNET, 8:1795

MARIE, 8:3450

MARSOT, 8:2133, 9:0176

MARTIN, 8:1887, 8:3251

MASSEY, 8:1768

MASSOT, 8:1753

MATHIEU, 8:3217, 8:3332

MATOUILLET, 9:0082

MATT, 8:3182

MATTHIEU, 8:2403

MAURER, 8:3039, 9:0325,
  9:0726

MAUSER, 9:0479

MEINSOHN, 8:2873,
  8:2890, 9:0764

MEISTER, 9:0092

MELLECKER, 8:2701

MENAGER, 9:0009

MERCKLEN, 8:2241

MERNNIN, 9:0485

METROL, 9:0034

METROT, 9:0034

MEYER, 8:1809, 8:1810,
  8:1862, 8:1958,
  8:2411, 8:2770,
  8:2928, 8:3140,
  8:3365, 9:0058,
  9:0182, 9:0245,
  9:0490, 9:0825

MEYLING, 9:0425

MINNIES, 9:0635

MISSLAND, 8:2362, 8:2764

MOETHER, 9:0220

MOHR, 9:0499

MOHR. See also MOURRE

MOINAT, 9:0231

MOINE, 9:0020

MONNIER, 8:3277

MONNIN, 9:0485

MONSHEIM, 8:2694

MORTEAU, 9:0611

MOUGEOT, 9:0514

MOUILLESEAUX, 9:0001

MOURNE, 9:0086

MOURRE, 9:0086

MOURRE. See also MOHR

MUECHLER, 8:1847

MUELLER, 8:3452

MULLER, 8:2229, 8:2507,
  8:3273, 8:3314,
  8:3452, 9:0637,
  9:0773

MUNCH, 8:3164

MUNSCH, 8:2144

MURINGER, 9:0791

MUSSLIN, 9:0780

MUTH, 8:1712

NAEGELIN, 8:3143

NAGEOTTE, 9:0657

NALDY, 8:2996

NASS, 8:1724

NEHR, 8:3211

NEUBAUER, 8:2865

NEUHART, 8:2161, 8:3086

NICOT, 8:3093

NIEDERKOHLER, 8:2857

NIEFERGOLD, 8:3301

NITTERKOLLER, 8:2541

NUDELHOFFER, 8:1815

NUN, 8:3059

OBERLAND, 9:0737

OBERST, 9:0075

OHR, 8:3119

ORRIEZ, 8:3446

PAIRIR, 9:0795

PARIS, 9:0606

PASSON, 9:0685

PAULIN, 8:1914, 8:3411

PAYOT, 8:2984

PAYSON, 9:0685

PECHIN, 9:0002

PEGUIGNOT, 9:0341

PELTIER, 8:3255

PEROT, 9:0436

PERRIN, 9:0698

PERROT, 8:2212, 8:3035

PETER, 8:3186

PETER. See also PETER
  (translation)

PETHER, 9:0568

PETREMENT, 8:3284

PEUGUET, 8:3291, 8:3292,
  9:0706

PFAFF, 9:0760

PFEIFFER, 9:0874

PFIESTER, 8:1791

PFISTER, 8:3181, 9:0573

PFLEGER, 8:2598

PFUESTER, 8:1791

PHILIPPE, 8:3396

PIERCON, 9:0725

PIERRE, 9:0673

PIERRE. See also PETER
  (translation)

PIQUEREZ, 8:2742, 9:0087

PONCE, 8:2631

POURCHOT, 9:0681

PRAUSS, 9:0358

PREBHAN, 8:2536

PRENAT, 8:2522, 8:2523,
  8:3099, 8:3100,
  8:3101, 9:0646,
  9:0649

PRENEZ, 9:0036

PREVOT, 8:3429, 8:3442

PRONEZ, 9:0036

PRONGUE, 9:0037

PRUD'HOMME, 8:3266

PY, 9:0667

QUICKERT, 9:0746,
  9:0747, 9:0761, 8:0762

RAETTICH, 9:0195

RAPINE, 9:0470, 9:0471

RAPP, 9:0011

RAUSS, 9:0358

REBER, 8:3483

REBHAN, 8:2536

REBISCHEN, 9:0433

REBISCHON, 8:2919

REBISCHUNG, 8:3184

REDELLE, 9:0021

REFFE, 9:0538

REICH, 8:2396

REISSER, 9:0851

REITTER, 8:2748

RELISCHUNG, 8:3184

REPERT, 8:1748

RESDEAMES, 8:2624

RESTLY, 8:1953

RESWEBER, 8:1716

REY, 9:0102

RIBER, 8:3071, 8:3072

RICH, 9:0829

RICH. See also RISCH,
  RITSCH

RICHARD, 9:0159, 9:0173,
  9:0235

RICHARDT, 9:0260

RICHERT, 8:2529, 8:3354

RIEGGER, 9:0816

RIEHL, 9:0360

RIGLY, 9:0615

RIOTTE, 9:0794

RISCH, 9:0587

RISCH. See also RICH,
  RITSCH

RISS, 9:0850

RITSCH, 9:0651

RITSCH. See also RICH,
  RISCH

RITTIMANN, 8:3114

RIVIERE, 9:0043

ROCHLY, 9:0517

ROGENMUSER, 9:0263

ROMOND, 9:0722

ROOS, 8:2410

ROSIER, 9:0310, 9:0313

ROSIET, 9:0032

ROTH, 8:2079, 8:2615,
  9:0614, 9:0824

ROTHMUND, 8:2189, 9:0694

ROTZELEUR, 8:1873

ROUECHE, 8:1886, 8:2538,
  9:0169

ROY, 8:2591, 9:0714

ROYER, 8:2732

VONAU, 9:0806

WAAG, 9:0126

WACKER, 9:0254

WADEL, 8:2595

WADENPFUL, 8:2188

WAGNER, 8:3132, 9:0781

WALCH, 8:3357

WALKRE, 9:0137

WALLER, 8:2713, 9:0789

WALLIS, 8:2719

WALTER, 8:1950, 8:2856, 9:0335, 9:0789

WALTZER, 9:0663

WAPLER, 8:2176, 8:2636

WEBER, 8:1790, 8:2387, 8:3200, 9:0593

WECKER, 8:2914

WEIDENPFUL, 8:2188

WEINGARTHNER, 9:0745

WEINMANN, 9:0124

WEINZAEPFLEN, 9:0502

WEISS, 8:2102, 8:2777, 9:0060

WEISS. See also BLANC (translation)

WELDY, 9:0743, 9:0744

WENDLING, 8:2514, 8:2843, 8:2931

WEPFER, 9:0148

WETZEL, 8:2579, 8:3199, 9:0719

WEY, 8:2805

WEYMANN, 8:3244

WICKERSHEIM, 8:1792, 8:2635, 8:3191, 8:3210

WICKY, 8:2379

WIEKERSHEIM, 8:2635

WIESER, 8:2810

WILD, 9:0496

WILL, 9:0368

WILLIAM(S). See GUILLAUME (translation)

WILLIEN, 8:2242

WINTER, 9:0815

WIPF, 8:3080

WIPFF, 8:3077

WIRTH, 8:2593, 9:0160

WITT, 9:0278, 9:0368

WITTMANN, 8:2512

WOHLSCHLAG, 9:0103

WOLF, 8:3218

WUEHLINGER, 8:2428

WUERLENSCHLAG, 9:0786

WURSTEISSEN, 8:2078

WUST, 8:3241

YANDOT, 8:1828

YARDOT, 8:1828

YETTER. See JETTER

YODER. See JODER

ZELLER, 8:2985

ZENGERLE, 8:2886

ZERR, 8:3214

ZIEGER, 9:0440

ZIMBIEHL, 9:0582

ZIMMERMANN, 8:2064, 9:0524, 9:0525

ZINSMEISTER, 8:3078

ZUERCHER, 8:3117

Note to Genealogical Researchers:

If you have immigrant ancestors, not listed in this monograph, about whom you have limited or no information, Westland Publications may be able to help you. We now have a computer listing of about 27,000 different surnames (with spelling variations) upon which we have emigration information, usually from European records. The list includes surnames from the following Westland series of monographs:

    British-American Genealogical Research Series
    French-American (Alsatian) Genealogical Research Series
    German-American Genealogical Research Series
    German and Central European Emigration Series
    American Genealogical Resources in German Archives (AGRIGA)

The information almost always includes the European place of residence, year, accompanying family members, and sometimes other information of genealogical interest, as well. Period covered is from the early 1700s to about 1860 with a few listings to the 1930s. AGRIGA entries pertain mainly to estate matters in which testators lived in Germany and their heirs in the United States.

Write to Westland Publications, Post Office Box 117, McNeal, AZ 85617-0117, for further information as to availability and cost of computer retrieval.